Naomi Ozaniec is a writer and teacher who has some twenty years experience in the contemporary Western Mystery Tradition. She has an abiding interest in Ancient Egypt and the priesthoods of the ancient world. Her books include *The Elements of the Chakras* and *The Element Tarot Handbook*.

W9-BNU-390

The *Elements of* is a series designed to present high quality introductions to a broad range of essential subjects.

The books are commissioned specifically from experts in their fields. They provide readable and often unique views of the various topics covered, and are therefore of interest both to those who have some knowledge of the subject, as well as to those who are approaching it for the first time.

Many of these concise yet comprehensive books have practical suggestions and exercises which allow personal experience as well as theoretical understanding, and offer a valuable source of information on many important themes.

In the same series

>> **the elements of**

the egyptian wisdom

naomi ozaniec

ELEMENT

Shaftesbury, Dorset · Rockport, Massachusetts · Melbourne, Victoria

© Element Books Limited, 1994
Text © Naomi Ozaniec 1994

First published in Great Britain in 1994 by
Element Books Limited
Shaftesbury, Dorset SP7 8BP

Published in the USA in 1994 by
Element Books, Inc.
PO Box 830, Rockport, MA 01966

Published in Australia in 199e by
Element Books and distributed
by Penguin Books Australia Ltd
487 Maroondah Highway, Ringwood,
Victoria 3134

Reissued 1998

All rights reserved.
No part of this book may be reproduced or utilized
in any form or by any means, electronical or mechanical,
without prior permission in writing from the Publisher.

Cover design by Max Fairbrother
Design by Roger Lghtfoot
Typeset by The Electronic Book Factory Ltd, Fife, Scotland
Printed and bound in Great Britain by
Biddles Ltd, Guildford and King's Lynn

British Library Cataloguing in Publication
data available

Library of Congress Cataloging in Publication
data available

ISBN 1–85230–497–9

ACKNOWLEDGEMENTS

I am deeply indebted to the works of Isha and R. A. Schwaller de Lubicz whose insights have been a great source of nourishment to me. I can only recommend that the readers discover these treasures for themselves. I am also indebted to the ideas expressed by Jane Sellers whose book struck me with great force the very moment I found it.

This book is dedicated to the priesthood of the Egyptian Wisdom. They know who they are. It is also dedicated to those who seek the Ancient Wisdom for there is a blessing upon those who quest in the spirit of truth.

CONTENTS

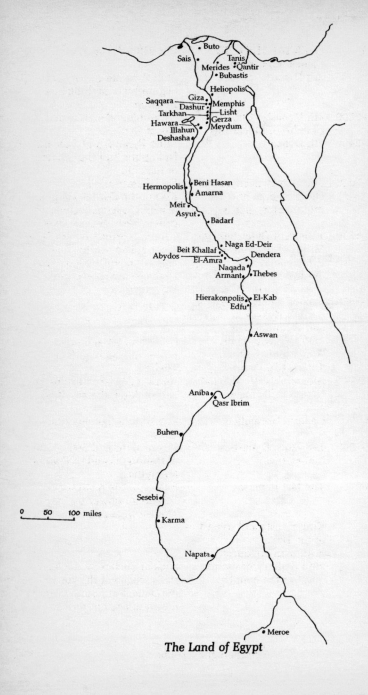

The Land of Egypt

DATE	OFFICIAL HISTORY	RELIGIOUS DATA
3000	Menes, First King.	
2800	3rd Dynasty: Djeser.	Step Pyramid of Saqqara; beginning of architecture in stone
2700-2600	4th Dynasty: Cheops, Chephren, Mycerinus.	Pyramids and private mastabas of Giza.
2600-2400	5th Dynasty.	Little Pyramids of Saqqara; Heliopolis and the religion of the sun.
2400-2000	6th-11th Dynasties: end of Old Kingdom and 1st intermediary period.	Social revolution. Rise of the Osirian religion, of which Abydos becomes the center. Sarcophagus texts.
2000-1750	12th-14th Dynasties: the Middle Kingdom, kings Amenemhat and Sesotris.	Pyramids of the Fayoum; Jake Moeris; Labyrinth; Appearance of the god Amon; vogue of the gods of the Fayoum.
1750-1580	Second intermediary period, Hyksos occupation and reconquest.	
1580	18th Dynasty: kings Amenophis and Tuthmosis.	Growth of the temporal power of Amon, god of Thebes.
1372-1343	Amenophis IV, Akhenaten, Nofretete, Tut-ankh-amon.	Heresy of Amarna: exclusive cult of Aton, the sun disc.
1343	General Horemheb.	Return to religious orthodoxy.
1314-1085	19th-20th Dynasties. The Ramessides.	Vogue of the god Seth, of Re of Heliopolis and of Ptah of Memphis.
1100	The last Rameses.	Pillage of the royal tombs. Seizure of power by the Theban high priests.
	King-priests and dynasties of the Delta.	
730	Ethiopian conquest.	
663	26th Saite Dynasty; reconquest of the country.	Sack of Thebes by the Assyrians; vogue of the gods of the Delta, Neith, Isis, Osiris; return to ancient forms.

Chronological Table

DATE	OFFICIAL HISTORY	RELIGIOUS DATA
525	Persian conquest.	Increasing importance of the cult of sacred animals and popular magic.
400-340	28th-30th Dynasties.	Reconstruction of the temples of Egypt.
341-332	Second Persian occupation.	
332	Conquest of Alexander the Great. Ptolemy kings.	Construction of the greatest temples: Edfu, Philae, Behbeit, Esna, Medamud, Kom Ombo, Dendereh. Cult of Serapis.
30 A.D.	The Roman province of Egypt.	
384 A.D.	Theodosius.	Closing of the temples of Egypt.

Chronological Table

The stellar universe is alive, directed by will and controlled by intelligence.

C. R. F. Seymour, The Forgotten Mage

Ancient Egypt did not have a 'religion' as such, it was religion in its entirety.

R. A. Schwaller de Lubicz, Sacred Science

Do you know then not know O Asclepius, that Egypt is the copy of heaven, or rather, the place where here below are mediated and projected all operations which govern and actuate the heavenly forces, even more than that, if the whole truth is to be told our land is the temple of the entire world.

Hermes Tristmegistus to Asclepius, Corpus Hermeticum

INTRODUCTION

Egypt still exerts a powerful hold on the imagination. The Tutankhamun Exhibition, which toured the world, drew crowds who patiently waited hour after hour to look upon the face of the boy-king. Sadly for many, the death mask of Tutankhamun has become a cliché, the sole symbol of a society obsessed with the afterlife. There is no doubt that Egypt continues to fascinate. Like Carter we see 'beautiful things' and we wonder about the guiding spirit of a civilization so foreign, so unfamiliar and yet so spectacular in its achievements. We are puzzled by Egypt's many gods. We are curious about the Egyptian mummy and mesmerized by the possibility of Egyptian magic. We are awed by the magnificence of Egypt. We are perplexed as we search in vain for the single key which might unlock its raison d'être. If we are to comprehend the moving Egyptian spirit, we have to suspend disbelief, as we would to understand any great drama. The Egyptian civilization was indeed a living drama. Its temples were the setting for sacred enactment which bound god, king and people. Its state rituals were cosmic pageants, its Mysteries were silent secrets. The players in this story were the divine intermediaries, the officials both sacred and profane, the builders and artisans and of course the gods. Let us then suspend disbelief as the curtain rises on the land of Khem.

If we are even to touch upon the essential Egyptian spirit, we need to abandon twentieth-century conceptions. We have

1

to try to think in another language by using another mind-set. We may have many questions about Egypt, but should not expect to find answers in forms that we readily recognize. The Egyptians did not construct their civilization for our benefit. The attempt to understand the Egyptian mind only in our own terms has led to a confusion about Egyptian intent. Because we have located only a few astronomical texts, it has been said that the Egyptians had a poor astronomical knowledge. This is a poor argument when the proof of astronomical understanding is writ large in monuments of stone. It has been said that the Egyptians were poor mathematicians, yet they were undoubtedly the teachers to Pythagoras. If we look only for that which we readily recognize, we will be sadly disappointed. We must be prepared to think laterally and to make bold leaps of the imagination. Egyptologists are confined by the limitations of their discipline – it is their job to record, to observe and to describe. We do not have to labour within these confines; our self-imposed task is to understand and enter the Egyptian mind-set. We are searching for Wisdom, an invisible abstract quality which like a potent yeast works invisibly from within to raise up the cultural level of a civilization. We must look for it everywhere indirectly; it cannot be simply uncovered or defined. Yet if we look beyond appearance, beyond form, we will sense its unifying spirit at work.

We can only breach the gap between ourselves and the Egyptian past if we abandon twentieth-century assumptions; we cannot impose them upon the past and we shall be grossly mistaken if we simply attempt to substitute contemporary concepts. We have a monarchy, the Egyptians had dynastic monarchy. We have churches, the Egyptians had temples. We have a priesthood, the Egyptians had a priesthood. We are simply deceived if we equate these past and present institutions. We can only touch upon the past if we give up the present.

We will meet a civilization very different from our own. It was built upon the model of cosmic order and actively sought Wisdom and cherished Truth. It created Beauty not by accident but by design, espousing the continuing life of the Spirit not as a fading hope but as a complete certainty. Perhaps we who

2

have lost our way in the maze of competing choices and who live surrounded by the utilitarian and mundane might be enriched by even a momentary vision of Wisdom and her children Beauty, Truth and Knowledge.

Our approach to this great and long-lived civilization is two-fold – we need to use both the intellect and the intuition. The intellect will take us into the structure of Egyptian spiritual practice. The intuition will take us beyond practice towards Egyptian intent. Egyptian history provides the framework for our approach and meditation provides the vehicle for the realization of the reader. If you are familiar with the meditative techniques, you will need no further bidding. The journeys await. If meditation is a new experience for you, use the text as a means of creating pictures in the mind's eye. Be prepared to experience the same journey more than once. When the journey comes to life you will surely know it.

It is my hope that you will truly touch this current, for it still lives. This is perhaps the first mystery that you will discover, but it will not be your last.

1 · THE FOUNDATION

There was a time when, in one small strip of the world's land surface, man achieved an almost total equilibrium with his environment and created a society as near perfect as he has so far been able even to dream about.

Michael Rice, Egypt's Making

We look back to the Greeks as being the cradle of Western civilization, but the Greeks looked to the Egyptians. Curiosity drove enquiring Greeks to Egypt and what they found was far more astonishing than they could ever have imagined.

The list of Greek travellers is as impressive as it is long: Homer, Solon, Thales of Milet, Plato, Oenopidis, Galen, Hippocrates and of course Pythagoras himself, all visited Egypt in search of Wisdom. It is curious how many of these Greek names are familiar as representatives of knowledge and wisdom. Yet how many Egyptian philosophers or sages do we remember? These Greek travellers found an ancient civilization headed by a divine king. Its temples were beautiful and mysterious. Its priests were experts in many fields, especially astronomy and geometry. Here was a civilization with its head in the stars. Strabo recognized that the priests were 'profoundly versed in the knowledge of celestial phenomena'. Pythagoras, perhaps the most famous ancient philosopher of all, spent many years in Egypt. Iamblicus, his biographer, reported that, 'He thus passed twenty-two years in the sanctuaries studying astronomy and geometry, and being initiated in no casual or superficial manner in all the mysteries of the Gods'. If we look at the Pythagorean legacy we see the Egyptian Wisdom for ourselves.

THE WISDOM OF PYTHAGORAS

Pythagoras considered most necessary the use of symbols in instruction.

Iamblicus, The Life of Pythagoras

The influence of Pythagoras has been substantial. His endurance is a testimony to the power of a deeply satisfying holistic philosophy. Pythagoras described philosophy as the desire for and love of wisdom. He defined a philosopher as 'a man who devotes himself to the contemplation of the most beautiful things'. For Pythagoras and the Egyptians who taught him this meant 'the survey of the whole heaven, and of the stars that revolve therein'. Order began in the heavens. Cosmic harmony was the model for earthly harmony, 'As Above So Below'.

Pythagoras established a metaphysical philosophy, a doctrine of unity which encompassed the spiritual and the physical, the heavens and the earth. He integrated psychology with political philosophy, astronomy with ethics, music with piety, geometry with divinity. He reconciled mathematics with metaphysics and spoke about reincarnation. His teaching followed the Egyptian model; the symbolic became the cornerstone of his approach. We find the symbol at the heart of the Egyptian civilization. We see the symbol at the heart of the Pythagorean teaching system. Pythagoras shows us the face of the Egyptian initiate. We remember Pythagoras, but forget who taught him.

The life and work of Pythagoras provides an important clue if we wish to understand the Egyptian Wisdom. The scope and range of his ideas shows us very clearly what was considered to be important in the life of the temple. Knowledge for its own sake was valued. The intellectual life was part of the spiritual life; the mental life was a reflection of the divine life. Pythagoras shows us an holistic philosophy – this too was an

5

essentially Egyptian perspective. The variety, complexity and multiplicity which we see never implied separation; unity was ever present.

What specialized knowledge does the contemporary priesthood bring to the world? In a first-hand account, Clement of Alexandria described the varied specialities of the temple Wisdom. He saw a singer, who had to know two books of Hermes, carrying a musical instrument. He saw the soothsayer who had to know the four astrological books of Hermes. He saw a scribe who had to know 'the writings which are called hieroglyphics, concerning cosmology and geography, the path of the sun, of the moon and the planets, the topography of Egypt and the description of the Nile, the prescriptions relating to sacred objects, to the places which are dedicated to them, the measures and utensils used in ritual'. He saw the *stolist* who had 'to know everything relating to the instruction of what is called "moschospragistical", knowledge of the marks of animals, and the ten precepts which relate to veneration of the gods in the country which includes Egyptian piety, treatises on fumigations, offerings, hymns, prayers, processions, feasts' etc. He saw the prophet, the chief of the temple, who had to know ten books and 'comprehends the totality of the priestly wisdom on the subject of the laws and the gods'. The books were the books of Thoth, the creator of the Wisdom of the temple.

In our fragmented world, knowledge has become fragmented. Mathematics, architecture, astronomy, music, philosophy, art and medicine are seen to be separate and quite distinct. Mathematicians do not mix with medical men, architects do not mix with astronomers – they have little to give each other. In the great temples all branches of learning were housed under the same roof, regarded as aspects of the single Wisdom. In our materialistic world, knowledge has become secularized. In the temple, knowledge was the manifestation of the divine wisdom. To acquire knowledge was to observe the divine at work; all branches of learning were divine. All diverse branches were encapsulated within the highest exaltation of knowledge, the Sacred Wisdom.

R. A. Schwaller de Lubicz reminds us that 'to know the

origin and matter of existence – such has always been the essential preoccupation of thinking humanity'. This was indeed the Egyptian preoccupation. As we attempt to pierce the veil placed over the Wisdom of the temple by the Egyptians themselves, we will come to know the name and work of Schwaller de Lubicz very well. As an Egyptologist working outside the confines of Egyptology, he and his wife Isha perhaps alone have combined research with insight. Their early work was dismissed out of hand by traditional academics, but their original conclusions have since gained reputable admirers. We too should lend an ear to these truly staggering insights if we want to understand the Egyptian Wisdom. When we really come to grasp the enormity, complexity, sophistication and brilliance of the Egyptian Wisdom we too will be staggered.

AS ABOVE SO BELOW

Celestial bodies provide the basic standards for determining the periods of a calendar.

The Encyclopaedia Brittanica

Our society has become insulated from nature – we are untouched by the elements 'and unaware of the sky above our heads. Astronomy is a rarefied and specialized science which has little impact on everyday life. We take our time from the television, the radio, the clock and the calendar. It is inconceivable that we should find ourselves floundering in time, uncertain whether the New Year had started or if the month had commenced. Our lives could not function without the certainty of measured time. We have lost contact with the stars as physical realities, as symbolic presences, and as practical timekeepers. There can be little doubt that the Egyptians looked to the stars in all three capacities.

We do not have to wrestle with the problems of determining the calendar as our forefathers did. Here was the prototype of the well-ordered society, the divine model for life on earth. The relationship between earth, moon and sun defined the year and the passing of time; the stars defined greater cycles.

Life in the heavens and life on earth were considered to be one, an indivisible unity.

Every civilization has to develop its own sense of time both social and liturgical. The repeating cycles of the moon make it a natural time marker – its phases are easily tracked and counted. The sun brings its own pattern too as the earth reaches the repeating solstice and equinox points. However the solar and lunar cycles do not tally. As measured by the moon, 12 synodic months are 11 days shorter than the tropical year which is the interval between successive passages of the sun through the vernal equinox. This discrepancy was a problem for every early society.

We know that the Egyptians observed the stars. It is impossible to say at what date this was regularized. Watching the stars was a priestly function. At both the temples of Esna and Edfu we find the 'hour watcher,' the *imy-wnwt* priest. The hieroglyphs for this title include an eye which is perhaps descriptive of the watching function. The inscription from the statue of the astronomer Harkhebi dates from the third century BC and reads as follows:

Hereditary prince and count, sole companion, wise in the sacred writings, who observes everything observable in heaven and earth, clear-eyed in observing the stars, among which there is no erring; who announces rising and setting at their times, with the gods who foretell the future for which he purified himself in their days when Akh (decan) rose heliacally beside Benu (Venus) from earth and he contented the lands with his utterances; who observes the culmination of every star in the sky, who knows the heliacal rising of every ... in a good year, and who foretells the heliacal rising of Sothis at the beginning of the year. He observes her in the day of her festival, knowledgeable in her course at the times of designating therein, observing what she does daily, all she has foretold is in his charge; knowing the northing and southing of the sun, announcing all its wonders and appointing for them a time, he declares when they have occurred, coming at their times; who divides the hours for the two times (day and night) without going into error at night ... knowledgeable in everything which is seen in the sky, for which he has waited, skilled with respect to their conjunction(s) and their regular movement(s); who does not disclose anything at all concerning his report after judgement, discreet with all he has seen.

The astronomer priest Harkhebi is described as being, 'wise in the sacred writings'. This clearly indicates that he was initiated into the Egyptian Wisdom.

STARS AND GODS

No other constellation more accurately represents the figure of a man.

Germanicus Caesar

Regular sky watchers would have learned early that the stars appeared to move upon a regular course. The vast figure-like constellation of Orion lies across the celestial equator. In about 7300 BC, the first stars of Orion rose after a two-month period of invisibility just before sunrise to coincide with the spring equinox. Jane Sellers, author of *The Death of Gods in Ancient Egypt*, states that 'it is certainly possible that Neolithic skywatchers may early on have recognized that the first stars of Orion's appearance coincided with the mid-point of the cycle's sunrise positions, and Orion's 'office' as herald of the sun god could have become related to heralding the sun god's rising on this date'. However the divine coincidence was doomed to eventually disappoint. At latitude 25° N all the stars of Orion had ceased to rise on the equinox by approximately 6700 BC. In skies further north this failure had occurred some centuries earlier.

Imagine for a moment that you have been given the task of explaining the displacement of a great constellation. This vast constellation so like a human was no longer in his appointed place. Is it possible that the mythology of Osiris refers directly to the observed behaviour of the constellation Orion during this historical period? After Orion had ceased to be the herald of the new year's sun, this function was served for a long time by Aldebaran, the bright eye of the constellation Taurus. Of course, this marker could not last indefinitely either – Aldebaran too slipped.

PRECESSION

I suggest that Orion's precessionally caused failure to appear in 'his place' at 'his proper time' gave rise to long centuries of an oral tradition of Osiris's death.

Jane Sellers, The Death of Gods in Ancient Egypt

Jane Sellers takes her lead from Hertha von Dechend and Giorgio de Santillana who together suggest that the world's great myths are of common origin; namely explanation, elaboration and fearful musings caused by the phenomenon of Precession. She suggests that the myth of Osiris is a myth of Precession. The earth is not perfectly spherical. As a result, the gravitational forces of the sun and moon upon the earth cause a 'wobble'. The earth's axis, like a spinning top, slowly shifts in relation to the starry background. Over a short period this precessional lag is imperceptible but over a longer period it has specific consequences. It has practical repercussions for civilizations engaged in serious stellar observation. The Precession gives rise to extremely long-term cycles and the earth's axis slowly shifts. Varying stars occupy the office of pole star through the millennia and every star within a 47° wide band surrounding the celestial equator will experience a change in declination which affects how specific star groups rise past the horizon. Precession is an inexorable movement which, like an invisible monster, removes cosmic markers in relation to each other. Yet even this pattern can be understood. The movement of the earth generated through precession is so minute that it takes twenty-six thousand years to complete this cycle. Once understood its vast cycle is no longer monstrous but proof of an even greater cosmic harmony. However some thousands of years may well have elapsed as the innocence of starry-eyed wonder was replaced by the dread of disappointment until at last the light of illumination dawned.

During this period is it possible that the recorded events of the heavens gave rise to the stories of the gods on earth? Is it possible that the priesthood created stories which acted both as an aide memoir for themselves and as a code for transmitting such knowledge in secrecy, generation to generation? It is not difficult to identify familiar mythical motifs in the perceived results of precessional movement. The god was murdered, cast adrift in a casket. The star was gone, taken into the netherworld. The god had disappeared, the search to find him must be undertaken. Might we also look to the heavens for the identity of other Egyptian gods?

SIRIUS

It is Sothis your beloved daughter who prepares your yearly sustenance in this her name of Year and who guides the king when he comes to greet you.

The Pyramid Texts

During the fifth millennium, the dawn rising of the star Sirius coincided with the Nile's flooding and the summer solstice. The Egyptians were not slow to put this heliacal rising to good use. It enabled them to regulate the lunar count. As the twelve lunar months fell short of the natural year, every two to three years a thirteenth intercalary month was introduced to keep the seasons in place. It is impossible to overestimate the importance of this discovery for the Egyptians. The heliacal rising of Sirius was far more than a solution to an old problem; it assumed mythic and symbolic qualities. Sirius became identified as Isis, Queen of Heaven. She was the wife and sister to Osiris-Orion who searched so diligently for the body when he disappeared. Isis was associated with Sirius from the earliest of times; she was called 'Sothis the great lady of *wp rnpt*', the opener of the year. Both goddess and star were loved by the Egyptians as the faithful, constant and loving companion.

There is something unique in a society which looks to the heavens for its model of life on earth. The stars embody a quality of transcendence not found elsewhere. The apparent stellar movements reveal the movement of the earth. The interrelationship between earth, moon and sun are complex. Yet the desire to understand life on earth as part of a greater cosmic whole is a compelling vision. Probing the heavens brings not merely understanding and knowledge, it also brings a true sense of awe which is at the heart of all spirituality. This sense of cosmic place was at the heart of the Egyptian

Wisdom. We, who have stood on the moon and journeyed into space seem immune to the spiritual dimensions of our quest. By contrast the earth-bound Egyptians never lost a sense of wonder – their gods were always cosmic by nature.

Star Stories

The Egyptians personified the life of the heavens in stories. Jane Sellers believes that 'the evidence is persuasive that the ancients once having discovered important data concerning movements of the sky and once having perceived some mystical connections in numbers, considered this knowledge sacred and wishing to preserve it in written form devised an encoding that would be understood by only an elite few'. We must ask ourselves if we detect the same relationship in other Egyptian myths. Jane Sellers poses the rhetorical question for us: 'Is it possible that early man encoded in his myths special numbers, numbers that reveal to initiates an amazing knowledge of the movement of the celestial spheres?'

The civil year incorporated five extra days to approximate the days of the natural year. These so-called epagomenal days were won by Thoth and were attributed to the children of Nut. Osiris was born on the first of the five days, Horus was born on the second, Set was born on the third day, Isis was born on the fourth and Nephthys was born on the fifth and last of these days. This simple story preserved an astronomical truth.

THE CONTENDINGS OF SET AND HORUS

A total eclipse is the most spectacular sight known to man for the most powerful source of energy in our lives is actually blotted out.

Jay M. Pasachoff, Hour of the Midday Night

How might a generation of dedicated skywatchers have remembered and reported the dramatic and terrifying battle between light and dark, the eclipse? Imagine if an unusually short period was marked by more than one of these great cosmic dramas. In the eighty-year period between 4867 and

4787 BC, there occurred three solar eclipses and
eclipse. Alarmingly the year of the first eclipse cor
with the period around the disappearance of Aldebar
equinoctial marker. A total eclipse is predicted to hav   en
visible on 27 July 4867 BC over the settlements of Badari,
Hammmiya and Mustagidda. A second eclipse is predicted
over the locations Badari, Diospolis Parva and Hermonthis
in 4849 BC. An annular eclipse is predicted for 4864 BC
at Hermonthis and Nekhen, Diospolis Parva and Abydos. A
total eclipse is predicted for the year 4787. Furthermore due
to differences in latitude the equinox sighting of Aldebaran
would have continued at Nekhen until 4788, the year before
the spectacular total eclipse. In Upper Egypt Aldebaran had
already failed to mark the equinox in 4866 BC. Would this
terrifying sequence of events, the spectacle of a cosmic battle
between light and dark, not be taken as a sign of the contending
of the gods themselves? Was the battle between Set and Horus
really a mythologized account of this historical period? Were
the events of the heavens truly the stuff of myth? Who can fail
to notice the eclipse imagery in the following extract:

> Come thou to me quickly,
> Since I desire to see thy face
> after not having seen thy face.
> Darkness is here for us in my sight
> even while Re is in the sky;
> The sky is merged in the earth
> and a shadow is made
> in the earth today.

> The songs of Isis and Nephthys

COSMIC CONNECTIONS

*What matters to Earth's inhabitants is that they should know
of their vital connections with the sky.*
        Isha Schwaller de Lubicz, Her-Bak, Egyptian Initiate

The long-standing impetus of this civilization was a stellar
one despite its obvious solar overlay. The pyramid was an

appropriate symbol for a society which included both the many and the few within its priesthood. Stellar knowledge as opposed to stellar observation belonged to the realms of the truly learned. The Egyptian Wisdom sought to encompass all. It reached out to the visible limits, to the stars, and attempted to embrace all in a holistic, utterly spiritualized metaphysical philosophy.

Accordingly every act had its significance both mundane and cosmic. When establishing a sacred site, harmony between earth and sky was of vital importance – the Egyptian mind-set would permit nothing accidental or random. All had meaning, all had significance, all revealed a purpose. Sir Norman Lockyer was the first to draw attention to the possible cosmic alignments of various temples in *The Dawn of Astronomy* which was published in 1894. Since his day, however, archaeoastronomy has emerged as a blended science. It is no longer revolutionary to believe that early civilizations had both the knowledge and intention necessary to align buildings with cosmic markers. Lockyer's conclusions anticipated the contemporary work of de Santallina and von Dechend – he too believed that the Egyptians understood the effects of precession. It is quite possible that Egyptology itself will be revitalized through new advances in the field of archeaoastronomy. We still have much to learn; our main barrier is simply one of belief. We find it almost impossible to accept that an early civilization might have developed a sophisticated and unique approach to cosmology. It is we who are diminished by this limitation of view.

STARS, STARS, STARS

The Egyptians measured the earth with great success.
E. M. Antoniadi, L'Astronomie Egyptienne

Egyptologists currently recognize eighty-one astronomical monuments which contain an obvious stellar connection. However we seem to be incapable of recognizing anything other than the most obvious. We recognize a ceiling when it depicts a star map, as in the case of the beautiful ceiling in the tomb of Senmut, architect and favourite of Hatshepsut. We recognize a ceiling when it shows a zodiac, yet we seem to be incapable of recognizing a stellar monument unless it is decorated with stars!

Our love affair with Egypt is enshrined in a single structure, the Great Pyramid at Giza. This single monument fascinates and tantalizes us. It seizes our imagination; its vital statistics command respect, its dynamics mesmerize. The statistics of construction are overwhelming and often repeated. Its alignment is extraordinary, each side is aligned with the true north, south, east and west. Its corners are almost perfect right angles. We should be truly impressed by the feat of social organization, engineering precision and architectural planning. We should also wonder at the intensity of purpose which inspired the building and moved millions of tonnes of stone. Yet we are bewildered; we are filled with images of arcane rites and esoteric possibilities. We choose to project our wildest fantasies onto this mountain of stone. Every theory imaginable has been proposed. The Egyptians would have laughed at our wild and undisciplined theories but they would have approved of the attempt to find the symbolic in the actual. Egyptian symbolism, however, had a purpose and a practical application. Indeed the proper symbol conveys a truth, it is not a scrap of artistic fancy.

Our word 'pyramid' is derived from the Greek *pyramis* meaning 'wheaten cake'. It is unfortunate that word has become so firmly embedded in our language, for it conveys nothing, except that the Greeks thought these structures resembled wheaten cakes. The Egyptians called these structures by the name *mer*, meaning 'the place of ascension', or 'the instrument of ascension'.

The Place of Ascension, also called 'The Horizon of Khufu', confuses us. We know that the pyramid tradition was part of a solar cult; accordingly the solar hill was a representation of the primeval mound, the place of new birth. The pyramid was the stairway to heaven – it expressed a metaphysical belief in stone and form. We know that the Horizon of Khufu was part of a royal mortuary tradition which included other kings and other sites. The mortuary complex characteristically included the offering temple, a covered causeway and a mortuary pyramid. The Giza site as a whole conforms to this pattern. In its own day the site contained other tomb and subsidiary pyramids, mortuary temples, and a covered causeway which led to valley temples at the water's edge. We know that the Great Pyramid was part of a slow evolutionary development. There were pyramids of various kinds at Saqqara, Daishur and Meidum. It is a mistake to view the Giza pyramids as being isolated architectural forms; they were part of a long-standing tradition of solar expressions and shared a great deal in common with earlier complexes. Yet it is impossible not to regard this single structure as being both the culmination and the unique expression of this tradition. As a pyramid it exceeds all other similar structures in quality of construction, as a mortuary complex it confounds us with its obvious absence of a royal body and as a solar image we are forced to take its stellar aspects into account. The sun, itself a star, has a dual identity.

Our attention has been sharply re-focused by two recent developments. Rudolf Gantenbrink discovered what is thought to be a hidden chamber in one of the pyramid's shafts when his motorised robot unexpectedly encountered a stone closure with copper handles. Concurrently, Richard Bauval and Adrian Gilbert have presented a ritual stellar explanation for the Giza complex. They suggest that the three pyramids mirror the three stars of the belt of Orion, and that the figure is completed across the landscape by other pyramids representing other stars of the constellation. Their explanation is closer to the Egyptian spirit than anything so far suggested by academic Egyptologists although the stellar implications have been ever present for those attuned to the stars. Within the pyramid, two shafts reach from the King's Chamber out onto the surface and two shafts also reach out from the Queen's Chamber but fall short of the surface. The southern shaft of the King's Chamber is aligned to Orion, the star of Osiris. The shaft from the Queen's Chamber is aligned to Sirius, the star of Isis. Bauval and Gilbert propose the ritualized rebirth of the pharaoh as the god-king destined to walk in the stars. This was after all the mer, 'the instrument of ascension'. Why should we be surprised by a ritual explanation of a deeply ritualized civilization?

This satisfying solution should not blind us to the Egyptian's brilliance for multi-levelled application. Once we see this site in a stellar context, we are free to ask new probing questions. What can be learned from studying the stars? Without the use of refracting or reflecting mirrors the stars cannot be magnified for observation. However individual stars may be viewed passing across a suitably inclined frame as a reference point in a highly sophisticated trigonometry of earth and sky. The stars were therefore used as a means of learning about the dimensions of the earth. Richard Procter, whose insight preceded those of Bauval and Gilbert, suggested additional stellar alignments. In *The Great Pyramid, Observatory, Tomb and Temple*, he argued that the pyramid was regulated during construction by stellar alignment. Procter claimed that the Descending Passage was aligned to the lower culmination of the star Thuban in the constellation of Draco. As the structure was built higher, this passage would eventually have become useless as an alignment for the north-south axis. However a second Ascending Passage intersecting the first, permitted the sighting of the reflected star image through a pool located at the junction of the two passages. Before the building was completed Procter believed that, truncated at the height of the Grand Gallery, the pyramid would have made an excellent observation platform.

Is it perhaps a coincidence that the Egyptians referred to the pyramids as the Place of Ascension and contemporary astronomers use the term Right Ascension as a co-ordinate for plotting the position of a star?

If we are to understand the Egyptian motivation we should not forget the framework which they set for themselves. They wanted to understand their own meaning against the great cosmic facts of space and time. They never forgot the stars, we should not either.

2 · THE COMPANY OF THE GODS – PUAT NETERU

In front of you, you will see a high Pylon Gate in which is a narrow door. As you stand in front of it a priest of Horus and a priest of Anpu will appear. They are you, and you are they, for are you not the guardian of your own inner door? Ask these priests for the Word that will admit you to Her temple.

C. R. F. Seymour, The Forgotten Mage

The Egyptan term *Neter* loosely translates as 'god'. The term does not carry our contemporary connotations but rather implies causal, universal power. Egyptologists being bound by the limitation of their profession are unable to offer more than a historical guide to the gods of the distant past. A metaphysician alone is able to recognize that the gods embody eternal cosmic realities, the gods never die. The *Neters* are eternal. At first sight we are bewildered and confused by the Egyptian gods. It seems impossible to untangle the complex divine web which the Egyptians created. However we may distinguish a hierarchy of three levels; the metaphysical, cosmic and terrestrial.

The Metaphysical Neters include Amun – the hidden one; Atum – potentiality and Ra – the universal principle. Neith the cosmic virgin mother is also included here. The Cosmic

Neters include Isis, Osiris, Set, Nephthys and Horus, Thoth, Anubis, Hathor and Nut. The Terrestrial Neters include Ptah, Amun-Min, Set, Anubis and Mut, the mother principle.

We have to make an enormous leap in understanding from our own monotheistic background if we are to comprehend this foreign and sacred world view. We are faced with a constant tension between the one and the many, between unity and multiplicity. It is perhaps our desire for precision and distinction that brings confusion. We want to understand the Neters through straightforward and separate categories. This was never the Egyptian way – they did not view the universe as a collection of closed compartments, all was interrelated, continuous and dynamic. A Neter might have several names expressing various forms of appearance. Typically the sun god Ra appeared through a variety of forms, each under a different name. The morning sun was Khepera, the noon sun was Ra, the evening sun was Tem. Each aspect of the one god was worshipped separately at different cult centres. A single god was known under many names to reveal the full range of divine functions. Isis was known as Menkhet in Memphis, Hert in Coptos, Ament in Thebes, Renpet in Crocodiliopolis.

The Egyptian gods took many forms appearing in a variety of guises including animal-human combinations. The Egyptian mind did not baulk at presenting the strangest combinations. The god Khepera, a form of the sun god, appeared with the head of a beetle, the god Horus-Set appeared with two heads, the strange ass-like head of Set and the familiar hawk head. The goddess Rennut had the head of a serpent. These varied and sometimes bizarre forms were part of an arcane iconography, a sacred symbolic code. How can we make sense of contradictions which defy logic? How can we approach an overpowering multiplicity of forms? How can we appreciate the extraordinary convolutions of the Egyptian religious mind? Where lies Wisdom?

SACRED SIGNS

The symbolique includes imaged writing as well as gestures and colours, all aimed at transcribing in a functional manner

> *the esoteric significance of a teaching whose inner meaning*
> *remains inexpressible by any other form.*
>
> R. A. Schwaller de Lubicz, Sacred Signs

It is possible to penetrate the seemingly impenetrable. We need to be guided by a handful of key principles rather than allow ourselves to become distracted by overwhelming particulars. The Egyptian psyche was attuned to the complexity and richness of symbolic thought. To the uninitiated the symbol served as a barrier, a closed door. To the initiated for whom the multiplicity of meanings had been revealed, the symbol is the key. We have to admit that we stand as non-initiates separated by several thousand years of historical development. Yet in truth we seek initiation into these arcane truths for we seek to understand the meaning expressed so artfully through line and form. We can only understand the Egyptian mind-set through the symbolic. All was symbolic, each stela and monument, every hieroglyph, each image and colour, all had a symbolic message. If we understand that all Egyptian iconography is a sacred code, we may at least view it through the proper perspective. The divine images are pictorial metaphors. The accoutrements of the gods are part of a sacred vocabulary. Sceptres and crowns, wands and wings are not mere poetic device but keys in a wholly symbolic sacred structure. We need to comprehend the symbol if we are to understand its function.

The most obvious Egyptian symbol is clearly the *ankh*, the looped cross. It means 'life or living'. The *ankh* is invariably carried and extended by the divinities. It represents the unity of spirit and matter which are never separated. This symbol carried a powerful message – manifest life shows forth divinity continuously and totally. The Egyptian never suffered from the great schism between spirit and matter, heaven and earth, which has done so much damage in our time. The *ankh* reconciles these polarities; it is truly the key to the Mysteries, the key to life.

A broad sweep through Egyptian iconography will reveal a wide range of sceptres and staffs. The contemporary sceptre still retains its link with regal authority, so the symbol is not

Ankh

entirely foreign to us. The most common symbol of authority is probably the crook and flail. The *heq*, the crook much like a bishop's crozier, gathers in. The flail, the *nekhakha*, symbolizes three aspects of being. These two symbols may be held with crossed wrists symbolizing death, with opposing fists symbolizing judgement or with crossed wrists and crossed sceptres symbolizing resurrection. The *heq* is held in the left hand, the receiving side, the *nekhakha* is held in the right hand.

Less commonly seen is a long cane with a curved top much like a long walking stick. The papyrus sceptre commonly held by Hathor signifies new life. The papyrus plant burst into new green life annually, while the papyrus plant itself and the colour green also signified the renewal of life. Osiris is often painted green. The *was* sceptre, 'the key of the Nile', draws its symbolism from the living branch cut in a particular way from the tree to conduct the ascending and vivifying sap – it

Crook and Flail

is therefore a symbol of creation. Its Sethian head evokes the concept of duality within manifestation. The heraldic staffs as a pair are crowned and entwined by the serpents of north and south. The *sekhem* baton denotes power and might. It is depicted in offering rituals. There are other more specialized sceptres which denote a particular function. One staff supports the *hb sd* symbols which are offered to the pharaoh. A pair of sceptres bears the twin goddesses Wadjet and Nekbet.

The *djed* pillar represents the principle of stability through the four elements. It is the backbone, the axis mundi. Its raising symbolizes the return to stable order.

The *was* sceptre, *djed* pillar and *ankh* were often depicted on a basket. This simple image of an everyday object signified 'all'. The sideposts of the temple's great entrance doors were often ornamented with horizontal bands of bas-reliefs portraying the three symbols. These three signs are usually read as 'prosperity', 'life' and 'stability'. They involve the three principles of beginning. We always have to align ourselves with the principles being represented if we are to understand the code through which we may come to know the Wisdom of Egypt.

It is impossible to convey more than a brief glimpse of this extraordinary system which bound god and king, nation and land into the synthesis of the living Wisdom. Revelation alone may convey the inner reality of Egypt to you. Words cannot describe the gods, the gods must describe themselves to you. Let the gods speak.

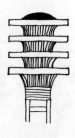

Djed

MAAT SPEAKS

I am Maat, Lady of the Judgement Hall. I stand upon the pedestal, the workman's cubit by which all is made straight. I am she who is straight. I am that which is straight. I am the straight rule, the rule of law. I am the upholder of divine law which is perfect truth and absolute wisdom. I am the cosmic order which is truth itself. I hold the sceptre and the ankh. I wear the white feather of truth.

I am partner to wise Thoth. Together we stand in the boat of Ra when it rises. Together we stand close to the royal house. The pharosh offers to me continually so that he shall not forget that he is the upholder of that whichis straight upon the earth. I am accorded a special place. I have been described as the 'most beautiful synthesis and highest philosophy of Egypt: Maat who impersonates Justice and Truth. All feminine Neters are aspects of the great divine Mother but Maat is at the same time her source and fulfilment. Ceaselessly emanating from divine Ra of whom she is at the same time herself the nourishment, she is the mediator and the vehicle of the essence of Ra. She is the Presence of beginning and end, in all Times and all Worlds. She is Cosmic Consciousness, Universal Ideation and Essential Wisdom.'
Isha Schwaller de Lubicz, *Her-bak – The Living Face of Egypt*

Maat

23

I am accredited with regulating the path of the sun. In this capacity I am called 'the daughter of Ra' and 'the eye of Ra'. On earth I exercise the moral law through the great house, the per aa, the phaaoh. I am justice. All law-givers and law-makers act in my name.

All will pass through the Hall of Maat. The deceased will face the Forty-Two Assessors and I will watch and wait, for I measure all in the weighing of the heart.

OSIRIS SPEAKS

I am Osiris, husband and brother of Isis. I was born upon the first of the five extra days. My names were many, Khnemu-ut-em-ankh in norther Nubia, An in Denderah, Seker in Memphis. At Mendes in the north I was called God of Top of the Steps. Yet I am one.

It was Plutarch, the good priest, who collected my story that you might know it. According to this tale I, Osiris as king of Egypt, applied myself towards civilizing my countrymen, 'by turning them forever from their former indigent barbarous course of life'. I 'taught them how to cultivate and improve the fruits of the earth'; I 'gave them a body of laws to regulate their conduct by, and instructed them in that reverence and worship which they were to pay to the gods'. When Egypt had

Osiris

become peaceful and prosperous I set out to instruct other nations of the world. In my absence Isis ruled alone. On my return, though I did not know it, my jealous brother Set had already plotted my death. 'Having first persuaded seventy-two other persons to join with him in the conspiracy' and 'having privily taken the measure of Osiris's body, he caused a chest to be made exactly of the same size'.

This chest was brought into the banqueting room. Set promised to give it to anyone who fitted within it. The whole company in turn lay within the chest but it did not fit any of them. Last of all I, Osiris, lay down in it, so eager was I to please my brother. At once the conspirators locked the lid shut. The chest became a coffin and I was cast into the sea. I passed into the Land of Light.

My beloved Isis set out to find my mortal remains. She received news that the chest had been carried to the coast of Byblos, where it had lodged in the branches of a Tamarisk tree which had since grown around it. The king of the country, amazed at its unusual size, had cut the tree down, and made it into a pillar to support the roof of the palace. Isis stayed at the court where she nursed the king's son and finally reclaimed the chest. However Set, not content with my death, came upon my body and tore my being into many parts. My beloved set out again. She honoured my body with burial. 'Wherever Isis met with any of the scattered limbs of her husband, she there buried it.' These mythical burial places became my sanctuaries. However my manhood was never found having been devoured by the Nile fish.

I became the Lord of the Underworld. My festivals showed the continuous round of life. I am eternity and everlasting-ness. I am the god of vegetation. I was dismembered. I was destroyed, yet I am. The month of Khoiak was mine. It was filled with remembrances of me. On the last day of the month the Djed pillar was set up. The populace witnessed my triumphant return in festival. The priesthood enacted my resurrection in private. At Abydos my underworld was created in the Osirion. Here my rites were celebrated. Remember my name for we shall certainly meet. I am Osiris. I am worshipped with warm words. I am hymned by those who love me. I, Osiris, Lord of the West, will not forget those who remember me.

Hail to you Foremost of the Westerners, Wennefer, Lord of the Sacred Land! You have appeared in glory like Re, and behold he has come to see you and rejoice at seeing your beauty.

His sun disc is your sun disc;
His rays are your rays;
His crown is your crown;
His greatness is your greatness;
His appearings are your appearings;
His majesty is your majesty;
His savour is your savour;
His extent is your extent;
His seat is your seat;
His throne is your throne;
His heritage is your heritage;
His panoply is your panoply;
His destiny is your destiny;
His West is your West;
His wisdom is your wisdom;
His distinction is your distinction;
He who should protect himself does indeed protect himself –
And vice versa.
He will not die and you will not die;
He will triumph over your enemies;
Nothing evil will come into being against him,
And nothing evil will come into being against you for ever
and ever.

Spell 181, Chapters of Coming Forth by Day

ISIS SPEAKS

I am Isis. I am called Ast. I came to birth upon the fourth of the extra days. I am she of the throne. I, Isis, was queen and wife to the murdered Osiris. You have already heard my tale. My sorrows were enacted by those who sought to awaken the heart. For my story is the story of all who seek. My son Horus was conceived between the worlds.

I am called a 'woman who was skilled in words'. For I know the secret name of Ra which he traded with me that

Isis

I might release him from the venom of the serpent. I alone could do this.

I wear the vulture cap and hold the papyrus sceptre and the ankh. I am crowned with horns surmounted by the solar disc. Sometimes I wear the double crown of south and north. I am seen with my beloved Osiris, with my son Horus, or in the company of my sister Nephthys.

I have many names. As earth goddess I am called Usert. As the goddess of the underworld I was called Thenenet. I was Sati, Anquet, Renenet, Ament. I had so many names that I was called Isis of Ten Thousand Names. I had many titles. I was called Divine One, the Greatest of the Goddesses, the Queen of all Gods, the Crown of Ra-Heru, Sept-Opener of the Year, Lady of Heaven, the Light Giver, Lady of the North Wind, Queen of the Earth and Benefactress of the Tuat.

My star was Sirius. My symbol was the *tet*, the knot which binds me to all my beloveds. The island of Philae was dedicated to me. Listen to my words and you may hear the inner call to come to me.

I am the mistress of every land, and I was taught by Hermes and with Hermes I devised letters, both the sacred and demotic, that all things might not be written with the same letters.

I gave and ordained laws for men, which no one is able to change.

I am the eldest daughter of Kronos.

I am wife and sister of King Osiris.

I am she who findeth fruit for men.

I am mother of King Horus.

I am she that riseth in the Dog Star.

I am she that is called goddess by women.

For me was the city of Bubastis built.

I divided the earth from the heaven.

I showed the path of the stars.

I ordered the course of the sun and the moon.

I devised business in the sea.

I made strong the right.

I brought together woman and man.

I appointed to women to bring their infants to birth in the tenth month.

I ordained that parents should be loved by children.

I laid punishments upon those disposed without natural affection towards their parents.

I made with my brother Osiris an end to the eating of men.

I revealed mysteries unto men.

I taught men to honour images of the gods.

I consecrated the precincts of the gods.

I broke down the governments of tyrants.

I made an end to murders.

I compelled women to be loved by men.

I made the right to be stronger than gold or silver.

I ordered that the true should be thought good.

I devised marriage contracts.

I assigned to Greeks and barbarians their languages.

I made the beautiful and the shameful to be distinguished by nature.

I ordained that nothing should be more feared than an oath.

I have delivered the plotter of evil against other men into the hands of the one he plotted against.

I established penalties for those who practise injustice.

I decreed mercy to suppliants.

I protect righteous guards.

With me the right prevails.

I am the Queen of rivers and winds and sea.

No one is held in honour without my knowing it.

I am the Queen of war.
I am Queen of the thunderbolt.
I stir up the sea and I calm it.
I inspect the courses of the sun.
Whatever I please, this too shall come to an end.
With me everything is reasonable.
I set free those in bonds.
I am the Queen of seamanship.
I make the navigable unnavigable when it pleases me.
I created walls of cities.
I am called the Lawgiver.
I bought up islands out of the depths into the light.
I overcome fate.
Fate hearkens to me.
Hail, O Egypt, that nourished me.

The Aretalogy of Isis

ANUBIS SPEAKS

I am the son of Nephthys and Set. I was not one of the gods born on the five additional days. Hearken to the wise words of Plutarch. He understands the function of a symbol. 'There remain the useful and symbolical qualities, one of which is found in some animals and both in many.' If you would understand my role look to the functions and powers of the dog. I am the jackal of the desert. My senses are sharp. I can

Anubis

detect the smell of death. The wild jackal eats flesh even when putrefaction has set in. I Anubis am the Neter of digestion, an essential function of life. As I will devour the flesh in decomposition so the sarcophagus is called the flesh eater. We are one and the same.

Plutarch offers you a further insight. He says of me, 'By Anubis they understand the horizontal circle, which divides the invisible part of the world which they call Nephthys from the visible to which they give the name Isis, and as this circle equally touches upon the confines of both light and darkness, it may be looked upon as being common to both and from this circumstance arose that resemblance which they imagine between Anubis and the dog, it being observed of this animal that he is equally watchful by day as by night.' He continues: 'Others are of the opinion that Anubis meant time, and that his denomination of *Koun* does not so much allude to any likeness which he has to the dog, though this be the general rendering of the word, as to that other signification of the term *breeding*; because Time begets all things out of itself, bearing them within itself, as it were in a womb. But this is one of those secret doctrines which are made more fully known to those initiated into the worship of Anubis.'

I Anubis am the great god of embalming. I am called Am Ut, dweller in the chamber of embalmment. As watcher in the place of purification, I was called Khent Sehet. I was the oversoul of all embalming priests. I enveloped the embalming priests when they intoned the ritual words. I was called Guardian of the Secret. The chief embalming priest was called 'Overseer of the Secret of the Place'. I am present at the tomb, for a priest calls upon me to be present. I will be present at the doorway of the tomb when the mouth shall be opened and you shall step forth in the body of light. I will embalm your body for I am the Guardian of the Secrets. In the embalming chamber you shall be changed. For I will speak the words of transformation that you will be liberated from the flesh. And I will embalm each part of your mortal being with great care leaving no part aside. And I will oversee the great transformation which is at the heart of my mystery.

I shall accompany you in the Hall of the Two Truths. I am

the Opener-of-the-Ways. I am called Governor of the Hall of the God. I will escort you to the balance and I will ensure that all is correct. I will examine the tongue of the balance. I will produce the heart for judgement. I will await the outcome and will take you into the future. Death is my realm. I will open the doors of the Netherworld for you. What I have done for Osiris I shall do for you and we shall surely meet.

I hearken unto your words:

In peace O Anubis! it goes well with the son of Re at peace with my Sacred Eye; may you glorify my soul and my shade, that they may see Re by means of what he brings. I ask that I may come and go and that I may have power in my feet so that this person may see him in any place where he is, in my nature, in my wisdom and in my true shape of my equipped and divine spirit. It shines as Re, it travels as Hathor. Therefore you have granted that my soul and my shade may walk on their feet to the place where this person is, so that he may stand, sit and walk, and enter into his chapel of eternity, because I am one of the entourage of Osiris, who goes by night and returns by day, and no god can be created when I am silent.

Spell 188, Chapters on Coming Forth by Day

HORUS SPEAKS

I am Hor, the face of heaven. My names are many. My forms are many yet I am one. I am called the Lord of Joy, the Lord of the Horizon, god of Light, He who is provided with stars, Lord of the Uraeus, Heir of his father, and the Beautiful Horus who overthrows his enemies.

I am seen in all the works of the skies. I am in the darkening of the sun and its new light, for my eye shall not be blinded for long. I am seen in the rising sun and in the sun at its zenith. I am seen in the high flying hawk. I am the Lord of the Horizon. I am the face above you. My eyes are the moon and sun.

The historian Horapollo provides you with an important insight into my nature. 'When they would signify God, or height, or lowness, or excellence, or blood, or victory, they delineate a hawk. They symbolize it God, because the bird is prolific and long lived, or perhaps because it seems to be

Horus

an image of the sun, very capable of looking more intently towards the rays of the sun than all other winged creatures: hence also physicians for the cure of eyes use the herb hawkweed: hence also it is that under the form of a hawk they sometimes depict the sun as lord of vision. And they use it to denote height because other birds, when they soar on high, move themselves from side to side being incapable of ascending vertically but the hawk alone soars directly upwards.'

Do not be confused by my many forms. The Horus Neter has three main forms: Horus the Elder called Haroeris, Horus son of Isis and Osiris and Harpocractes. Horus the Elder is referred to as the son of Geb or Atum. Horus as the son of Isis and Osiris is the grandson of Geb and the legitimate heir to the throne.

I am the royal god. Menes, founder of the first dynasty, took a Horus name. All other kings followed him. I am the divine falcon, the protector of kings. I rest about his shoulders in my falcon form. I am upon the pharaoh, the great house and the pharaoh dwells in me. I am the protector of the great house. I bestow rightful descent upon the son of the father. The united lands were accorded to me after my battle. I am called Harsomtus, the uniter of the two lands. I am the true lineage. I am the rightful heir to my father. I am seen in the rising sun. I am the son of the sun. I Horus address the pharaoh, the great house. 'My sole sun, my heir upon earth, Lord of the two Lands, Lord of Strength. I rejoice greatly at seeing thy beauty. I am pleased with deeds which thou hast performed for me; mayest thou endure upon earth as king of eternity, mayest thou be stable like the Double Horizon.'

I am the conqueror of Set and the avenger of my father. I uphold my father. My festivals were those of victorious triumph. Did I not bring victory! My drama was performed beside a stretch of water. My people re-enacted the eternal battle between the light and the dark. My mystery included boats, weapons, clothes, masks, models of hippopotami and crowns. All was made real. The battle was joined with great gusto.

> Ho Osiris! I am your son Horus; and I have come to you that I may greet you my father Osiris.
> Ho Osiris! I am your son Horus; I have come having felled your enemies for you.
> Ho Osiris! I am your son Horus; I have come that I may remove all evil which is on you.
>
> Spell 173, Chapters on Coming Forth by day

THOTH SPEAKS

I am Thoth, Lord of Wisdom. I was not one of the gods born on the five extra days. Indeed it was I who, by my great power, was seen to win these five days in a game of chance. I am self created. I am a Neter of a different order. I am the teacher of Isis, herself an embodiment of the ancient Wisdom. Do you seek me for I am ever present? I am the god of Wisdom. All scribes of all the ages are my servants. I carry the scribal palette just like my servants. Those who seek to know truth are in my retinue. I am called Lord of the Divine Words and Lord of Maat. I bring the thirst for cosmic truth. I am the originator of all the arts and sciences; mathematics, writing, astronomy, geometry and medicine. The scribes of the House of Life were especially under my care and guidance. I am the Lord of Books.

Thoth

I breathe into my priesthood that they may hear my words. My priesthood receives 'the words of Thoth'.

I am Thoth, the skilled scribe whose hands are pure, a possessor of purity, who drives away evil, who writes what is true, who detests falsehood, whose pen defends the Lord of All; master of laws who interprets writings, whose words establish the Two Lands.

I am Lord of Justice, one truly precise to the gods, who judges a matter so that it may continue in being; who vindicates him whose voice is hushed; who dispels darkness and clears away the storm. I am Thoth, the favoured of Re; Lord of strength who ennobles him who made him; great magic in the Bark of Millions of Years; master of laws who makes the Two Lands content; whose power protects her who bore him; who gets rid of noise and quells uproar; who does what Re in his shrine approves.

I am Thoth who made Osiris triumphant over his enemies. I am Thoth who foretells the morrow and foresees the future, whose act cannot be brought to naught; and who guides sky, earth and the Netherworld, who nourished the sun-folk. I give breath to him who is in the secret places by means of the power which is on my mouth and Osiris is triumphant over his enemies.

I am Thoth; I have pacified Horus, I have calmed the Rivals in their time of raging; I have come and have washed away the blood, I have calmed the tumult and I have eliminated everything evil.

I am Thoth; I have come today from Pe and Dep, I have conducted the oblations, I have given bread offerings as gifts to the spirits.

I am Thoth; I have come today from Kheraha, I have knotted the cord and sent out the ferry boat in good order, I have fetched East and West, I am uplifted on my standard higher than any god in this my name of him whose face is on high; I have opened those things which are good in this my name.

Spell 182, Chapters on Coming Forth by Day

I was closely allied to the throne. I established the titulary of the king and guaranteed his legitimacy. I was the archetypal law maker. Menes the first king received his laws from me. My mysteries stood behind the Egyptian civilization as the unseen presence behind a great throne.

I was worshipped in Hermopolis called Khemennu. My temple here was called the Het Abtit, the House of the Net. A net was kept in my temple. I am he who reckons in heaven, the counter of the stars, the enumerator of the earth and of what is therein, and the measurer of the earth. I am the heart of Ra. I am the tongue of Ra. I help direct the Boat of Millions of Years with Maat, Lady of The Judgement Hall. I am the Wisdom which is Egypt. My Wisdom is Eternal. I am the Ancient Wisdom.

HATHOR SPEAKS

I am Ht-hr, The House of Horus. I am the womb of Horus. I am a sky goddess, mistress of the nocturnal sky. I am called Mistress of the Sky, Queen of the Stars, Ruler over Sirius, the Great One who makes the Nile come. I am the eye of Ra, Queen of the Gods, Possessor of Maat. I am seen in the living tree in a land where trees were scarce. My tree was the sycamore. I am nb.t nht, Mistress of the Sycamore.

I am depicted as a woman with cow's ears. I am also seen in purely bovine form as the wild untamed cow found in the marshy delta. Sacred cows were kept at my temples. In my prehistoric form, I am shown with stars at the ends of my horns and on my ears and forehead as well. I wear a sun

Hathor

disc ornamented with the uraeus and two horns. Sometimes I wear the vulture cap, borrowed from my sister Mut. My image is mirrored through my priesthood. As my epiphany, my priestesses bear the menat, the beaded collar and the sistrum. As they danced they called upon me and I cloaked them within myself.

I am a receiver of the dead. I am called *nb.t smj.t*, mistress of the western desert, the necropolis. The deceased prides himself on entering my retinue. Under my guardianship a banquet was held. The deceased were offered flowers, a sistrum and a necklace.

I had my own temple at Denderah. It was called the Castle of the Sistrum and the House of Hathor the *Per Ht-hr*. There was a chapel on the roof called the Chapel of the Disc. It had no permanent roof. Instead a wooden covering was drawn back so that my statue could receive the rays of the sun during the festival of Re.

There were many annual festivals in my honour. My effigy was taken from the temple and carried among the people. My greatest festival was my voyage to Edfu where I visited my beloved Horus for 'the festival of the beautiful embrace', *hb n shn nfr*. People delighted to see my flotilla processing upon the Nile; I showed them beauty and brought divine grace. My public festivals were full of joy and laughter. At the Festival of

Plucking Papyrus, people joyfully picked papyrus among the groves.

I was hymned with beautiful words:

> Hathor, Lady of the West; She of the West; Lady of the Sacred Land; Eye of Re which is on his forehead; kindly of countenance in the Bark of Millions of Years; a resting place for him who has done right within the boat of the blessed who built the Great Bark of Osiris in order to cross the water of truth.
>
> Spell 186, Chapters on Coming Forth by Day

I was a royal goddess. I assisted at the royal birth and suckled the child. Only through my divine milk might the young prince become a true king. See me in the mammesi, the birth house at Denderah. The royal son is under my protection. The pharaoh never forgot me and calls himself the oldest son of Hathor. At the festival of the *Hb Sd*, I attended the erection of the Djed pillar. I stood behind the pharaoh. The pharaoh sang to me with sweet words.

I am often seen in royal tombs. My beloved Queen Hatshepsut was my devotee. I spoke to her: 'I am thy mother who formed thy limbs and created thy beauty.' I am mistress of the dance, the queen of happiness, mistress of inebriety, of jubilation and of music. My son Ihy is the divine dancer. Beauty is my delight. Dance and feast in my name. Uphold beauty and I will walk among you.

NEPHTHYS SPEAKS

I am Nephthys, daughter of Seb and Nut. I am also called *Nebt-het* or *Nebkhat*. I was born upon the fifth of the extra days. I am the mother of Anubis. My name means Lady of the House. I am called Dweller within Senu, Lady of Heaven, Great Goddess, Lady of Life and Mistress of the Gods. I am seen wearing the horns and solar disc upon my head. I bear my symbol upon my head. I carry the papyrus sceptre.

I am inseparable from my sister Isis. She represents generation, I represent dissolution. Where Isis is light, I am darkness. When Isis represents what is manifest, I am that which is invisible and yet to come into being. Together we represent the

Nephthys

complete cycle of being. Accordingly the sistrum is engraved with our faces upon each side that people should not forget the two sides that make the whole.

We were the divine mourners. All mourners followed our practice. The two official mourners who accompanied the funeral cortège were called the two kites, which we ourselves were called. In the cultic mysteries of Osiris, two priestesses took our place as mourning women. Hear the words from the drama of Osiris.

Behold now, Nephthys speaketh –
Behold the excellent sistrum bearer! Come to
    thy temple!
Cause thy heart to rejoice, for thy enemies are not!
All thy sister-goddesses are at thy side and behind
    thy couch,
Calling upon thee with weeping – yet thou art
    prostrate upon thy bed!
Hearken unto the beautiful words uttered by us
    and by every noble one among us!
Subdue thou every sorrow which is in the hearts of us thy
    sisters,
Oh thou strong one among the gods – strong
    among men who behold thee!
We come before thee, Oh prince our lord;

38

Live before us, desiring to behold thee;
Turn not thou away thy face before us;
Sweeten our hearts when we behold thee, oh
   prince!
Beautify our hearts when we behold thee!
I, Nephthys, thy sister, I love thee.

> Ritual words spoken by the priestess taking
> the role of Nephthys in the Osirian drama.

SET SPEAKS

I am Set the red one. I was born on the third of the five days.
I was cast as the murderer of Osiris. I became the hated one.
I have been given few words to say for I am the reviled one.
All that is barren and fruitless, parched and without possible
life is given to me. I am depicted as a dog-like animal with a
long tail and long ears. I am often painted red which is the
destructive heat of the summer.

It was declared I stole the light from Horus. I personified
the dry stony lands. Plutarch says of me, 'they hold him in the
greatest contempt and do all they can to vilify and affront him,
hence their ignominious treatment of those persons whom
from the redness of their complexion they imagine to bear a
resemblance to him'.

I was one of the two combatants, one of the two brothers. I
fought for the throne of the two lands but it was not awarded to

Set

me. Yet we were well matched in battle. I was not defeated by force of arms. Our battle was long and hard. I tore out the eye of the sun and brought darkness. Great was my power, yet I was not granted dominion over the Two Lands. However, before this great battle, I was respected. We were described as twins. I helped the deceased ascend to heaven. Spell 50 speaks of my loss: 'The four knots are tied about me by the guardian of the skies, he has made the knots form for the inert one on his thighs on the day of cutting off the lock of hair. The knot was tied about me by Set in whose power the Ennead were first before uproar had come into being.'

Nevertheless my power was acknowledged for I continued to tie the knot of the Two Lands with my combatant-brother Horus. I was god of the south and Horus was god of the north. We were both present at the coronation ceremony being represented by our priests. We each poured a libation for Pharaoh Seti I. We both crowned Rameses II. I spoke unto him: 'I establish the crown upon thy head even the disc. I will give thee all life and strength and health.' We each held the renpet, the tally of the years.

Are you surprised that I should be shown teaching Thotmes III the use of the bow? With my brother-combatant, I continued to tie the Ligature of the Two Lands, an act of high honour.

Yet I have been given few words to say. I have no words of advice for the weary, no crumbs of comfort for the deceased. I have no words of wisdom to offer. Yet I do possess a secret which can only be fathomed if you look to the skies.

Expect nothing from me but silence, though you may penetrate my mystery if you have a mind to discover it. I will point your attention towards the heavens but more than that I will not do.

O ye gods who ferry over on the wing of Thoth, to that side of the winding canal, to the east side of the heaven, to intercede with Set for the eye of Horus: may the King ferry over with you on the wing of Thoth, to that side of the winding canal, to the east side of the heaven. May the King intercede with Set for that eye of Horus.

Pyramid Text 595a

3 · THE SERVANTS OF THE GODS – HM NETER

Do the monthly office of priest, don white sandals, enter the temple, open the secret places, tread the holy of holies, and eat bread in the house of the Lord.

The Wisdom of Merikare

The temple was the house of the god. The priesthood were the servants of the god, the *hm ntr*. We should not be deceived into thinking that we might simply transpose the functions and aims of our contemporary priesthood onto this ancient body. Pastoral care and the confession of sins was no part of daily life. The priesthood looked after the god, and if the god was properly treated the land and people would prosper.

The priesthood was organized into a hierarchical pyramid structure. At the head was the High Priest. Each cult employed its own titles for this office. The High Priest of Ptah at Memphis was called 'Great Chief of the Artisans'. The High Priest of Amun was called 'He who is permitted to gaze on the Great God'. The High Priest of Re was called 'He who is great at seeing'.

At the base of the power structure was the rank of the *wab* priest, 'the purified one'. This role was often filled by members of the lay priesthood who were organized into groups which ed for a month at a time. At the end of the month complete inventories were made out to ensure that all was in good order. Some small temples were manned entirely by these lay priests. Between the part-time lay personnel and the permanent High Priests lay a whole range of specialist functionaries. Below the High Priest came the 'Fathers of the God', the second, third and fourth prophets. Among the higher ranks of the permanent clergy was the rank of kheri-heb, 'the possessor of the book'. These priests were also described as 'lector priests'. The Greeks described them as pteroforoi, 'winged ones', in reference to the double plumes worn to signify rank. The kheri-heb was the archetypal Egyptian priest, shaven-headed and draped with a leopard skin. These priests played a central role in all state ceremonies and mystery dramas. They were initiated into the House of Life as the holders and keepers of the priestly Wisdom, unlike the lower priesthood who simply performed liturgical duties.

The Neter dwelt in the temple, the divine presence being immanent in the cult statue. The statue was clothed and cared for by the stolist priest, known as the medjty or chendjouty, 'the priest of the private clothing'. Other specialists were the horoskopoi who were familiar with the mythological calendar, dream interpreters called oinercrites by the Greeks, and temple musicians. There were also the sem priests who performed the funerary rite, 'Opening the Mouth; the funerary priests, hm ka, 'the servant of the ka' and the 'hour men of the god', the astronomer priests. At Karnak the personnel had as many as 125 functions.

The female priesthood held high status and had its own power holding offices. The chief priestess was often married to the chief priest and she exercised authority over the group of musician-priestesses. The cult of Hathor had its own unique hierarchy which gave considerable power and autonomy to women.

What can we learn about the Egyptian Wisdom from this organization? We need to distinguish between the many officials and administrators who clearly maintained the temple as a machine and the small number who, as lifelong servants of the gods, maintained the inner life of the temple. We have a classic example of the many and the few, the esoteric and the exoteric community living together.

The Egyptian High Priest was not a theologian but an expert in a particular field of knowledge. The Wisdom of the Temple produced priest-architects, priest-astronomers and priest-doctors. We do not expect our priests to be architects or doctors, judges or astronomers. Berenkhons, the High Priest under Amenophis III, was the chief architect who laid out Thebes with obelisks and trees. Here is a pattern we will meet repeatedly. The various priesthoods followed the speciality of their patron divinity. The scribe-priests, whether great or small, were in the service of Thoth, the god of Wisdom. The medical-priests were in the service of Sekhmet. The priests of the scorpion goddess Selkit specialized in treating the results of venomous bites. The priesthood of Imhotep, the deified scribe, were dedicated to the healing arts. The embalming priests were in the service of Anubis. The priests of Maat administered justice. The priestesses of Hathor were famed for their sacred song and dance. Each separate priesthood developed its own speciality; in this way knowledge was furthered and transmitted generation to generation. Yet the essential unity between various fields of knowledge was never lost. The spirit of synthesis, Wisdom, was ever present.

SAGES AND WISE MEN

The great medicine man, hk of Mehyt the Ancient. Prophet of Min. Carpenter of royal Science, royal scribe. Grand Master of the fly, Father of Min, Carpenter of the lioness. Great of the city of Pe, Chief of the guides. Great of the Ten of Upper-Egypt. Priest of Horus of Mesen of the city of Pe, Hesy.

The titles of the Sage, Hesy

There is no doubt that the Wisdom tradition produced its famous wise men and sages who were respected in their own lifetime. The Third Dynasty sage Hesy was honoured with archaic title. His name was written by two purification vases meaning 'twice blessed'. According to his titles, Hesy was in the service of Mehyt, an ancient lioness goddess who like

43

Sekhmet presided over the healing arts. His title 'Great of the Ten of Upper Egypt' referred to the ten judges who composed the highest court of justice under the aegis of Maat. Hesy was clearly a priest, a doctor, a judge and much more besides. The combination of the sacred and the mundane, the priest and the expert is a recurring theme. It is the practical product of the Wisdom tradition. Wisdom is not an empty abstraction but an empowering foundation. Who might we look to as current sage or wise man? Contemporary society does not produce servants of Thoth, only servers of self.

The sage Petosiris was however a High Priest of Thoth. He was venerated even in his lifetime and after his death his tomb became a centre for pilgrimage. As High Priest he bore the honoured titles 'seeing the Lord in his Naos, supporting his master, following his master, entering the holy of holies, exercising the priestly functions in the company of the great prophets, prophet himself of six primary gods, chief of the Sekhmet priests, chief of the third and fourth class priests and royal scribe responsible for all the goods of the temple of Hermopolis'. His tomb was inscribed with a plea to the generations yet to come. He cannot have known that his words would survive thousands of years.

Oh you living . . . if you listen to my words, if you heed them, you will find their worth. It is good, the path of the one who is faithful to the Lord; he is blessed whose heart turns towards this path. I will teach you what befell me, I will teach you the will of the Lord, I will make you enter into the knowledge of his spirit.

Oh you living, I will have you know the will of the Lord. I will guide you to the path of life, the good path of those who obey God: happy is he whose heart leads him towards it. He whose heart is firm in the path of the Lord, secure is his existence on earth. He who has in his soul a great fear of the Lord, great is his happiness on earth.

It is useful to walk in the path of the Lord, great are the advantages reserved for him who follows it. He will raise a monument to himself on earth, he who follows in the path of the Lord. He who holds to the path of the Lord, he will pass all his life in joy, richer than his peers. He grows old in his own city, he is a man respected in name, all his members are as young as an infant's. His children are numerous and looked upon as first in the city; his sons succeed him from generation to generation. He comes finally to the city of the dead, joyfully, finely embalmed by Anubis, and the children of his children live on in his place ... You have walked in the path of your master Thoth; thus, after having received the favours he grants you on earth, he will please you with like favours after death.

The last line of his temple inscription reads, 'May he who comes hereafter say, a servant of his god till veneration day'. Indeed this prophecy has been fulfilled.

THE SERVANTS OF HATHOR

Pythagoras was likewise of the opinion that music, if properly used, greatly contributed to health.

Iamblicus, The Life of Pythagoras

The cult of Hathor can be traced back to the Old Kingdom. It was filled almost entirely by women. Men were few in number and held only administrative posts. Women held the positions of authority and exercised responsibility through their own hierarchical structure. Hathor had her own temples, though only one has survived.

The Egyptians believed that both sound and movement had subtle effects on the emotional, mental and spiritual levels. Pythagoras understood this too from his stay in Egypt but the real experts in this field were the priestesses of Hathor. It seems pointless to compare the priesthood of Hathor with the role currently assigned to women in the church today. Women today seek to become priests not priestesses and the public ministry of the female as epiphany is impossible, probably even thought blasphemous. These servants of Hathor were the living epiphany of Hathor herself. Currently the priest is Christ's representative on earth; the priestess of Hathor was Hathor herself. Our quest for the rational and the intellectual has created a rift which the Egyptians could not even begin to fathom. We live in a mind-set dominated by notions of separation. We live in a world of specialists and specializations. At last we have become so sickened by this fragmentation that we too yearn for a holistic philosophy. The Egyptians were never deceived into elevating the rational mind above all else. The beautiful was as important as the rational; the *ka* was nourished by beauty expressed through sacred sound and gesture. Movement and sound had a secret power of themselves; these too were expressions of the divine principles. Goddess and priestess as one bestowed joy, beauty and grace, divine rapture and bliss. At festivals these musician-priestesses processed through the streets offering the extended *menat* to confer the blessing of life, stability and happiness upon the eager and devoted crowds. In the temple these musician-priestesses sang and offered sacred dance. The priestesses of Hathor were dressed as the goddess herself with the beaded collar, 'the divine *menat*' and the *sistrum*, the sacred rattle. It is probable that entry into the service of Hathor was marked by the bestowing of her ritual emblems. The ceremonial giving of the *menat* and *sistrum* conferred the right to walk in the service of Hathor and become her living garment. Sacred dancers attended both private funeral rites and pharaonic state rites; such dance was not designed to entertain or amuse but to evoke particular cosmic principles. The current religious mind-set could not permit a procession of women, adorned as an evocation of beauty, scented by perfume cones, to sway as one in perfected dance step as an honouring of the divine. Sacred beauty has been destroyed and defiled along with the destruction of pleasure and hatred of the body. Once again the cult of separation has claimed its victims and the loss of course is ours. Wisdom has been reduced to orthodoxy, holistic spirituality has became narrow religious observance. The priestesses have become invisible.

THE DAILY RITUAL

I have purified my breast and body with clean water.
Temple Inscription

We cannot really gain a full picture of temple life. The heart of this life lay in the unrecorded moments of realization, revelation, contemplation and adoration. We can only observe and describe the routine and the rituals. We can only guess the feelings and intentions of those who followed in this tradition century after century. The inner life of the temple still evades us. The outer life is adequately recorded. Each temple followed its own mythic calendar according to its presiding deity. The priesthood whether large or small, wealthy or poor served the god through the daily ritual which vivified the life of the temple. The heart of the priesthood lived as the epiphany of the divinity, exemplifying the special skills, aptitudes and attributes of the divinity. The Neter was made manifest through those who served the Neter.

Temple life revolved around the three daily services and the annual festivals which were performed with as much or as little pomp and ceremony as the wealth and significance of the temple permitted. The three daily services took place in the morning, afternoon and evening. The temple day began early. The watcher on the temple roof gave the signal which brought the temple to life. Even before dawn an immense amount of preparation had already taken place. The priests had been to the sacred lake to wash and purify themselves. Two priests had filled the libation vessels from the sacred well. Scribes appeared with offering lists for the day. In the abattoir and the kitchens, staff prepared offerings. Fruits and vegetables were heaped on offering plates. At the appointed moment the offerings were carried through the door in the enclosure wall into the temple proper. The bearers withdrew. The priests purified and consecrated the offerings which were then taken into the Hall of Offerings. Libations were taken into the Hall of the Ennead and offered up to the gods. Meanwhile the officiating priest, having made the declaration of innocence, and having been ceremonially purified in the House of the Morning, processed in solitary state to the sanctuary. It was he who broke the clay seal on the shrine and opened the doors to uncover the face of the god as the sun appeared above the horizon.

The chanter intoned:

Rise thou Great God, in peace! Rise, thou art in Peace.

From the answering chorus came the reply:

> Thou art risen, thou art in peace; rise thou beautifully in peace, wake thou, god of this city, to life. The gods have arisen to honour thy soul, O holy winged disc who rises from his mother Nut. It is thou who breaks thy prison of clay to spread on the earth thy powdered gold, thou who rise in the east, then sink in the west and sleep in thy temple each day.

The invocations continued passing back and forth between the chanter and the chorus. The great opening of the day continued:

> Thine eyes cast flame. Thine eyes illuminate the night. Thy brows wake in beauty, O radiant visage which knows not anger.

The divine body was awoken through forty-five invocations. Each invocation was answered by the refrain:

> Thou art risen, thou art in peace; rise thou beautifully in peace, wake thou, god of this city, to life.

Meanwhile the priest entered the sanctuary alone. He lit the candle of the day and broke the clay seal on the naos. He adored the divinity by contemplating the divine image and presented myrrh. A short embrace followed in which the priest placed his hands on the statue in order to 'give the god back his soul'. The god resumed his earthly resting place. The priest dropped his arms in respectful humility and repeated the formula four times.

> I worship thy Majesty, with the chosen words, with the prayers, which increase thy prestige, in thy great names and in the holy manifestation under which thou revealed thyself the first day of the world.

Incense was offered. The offering of Maat was made. The food offerings were withdrawn. The priest withdrew. Finally the stolist, 'the one who enters the sanctuary to dress the gods with their apparel', began his task. The god was washed and dressed with fine linen. Four strips of linen – white, blue, green and red – were placed in a casket. The full cult clothing was not renewed daily but weekly. The symbolic offering of strips was sufficient on a daily basis. The toilet of the god ended with anointing. The stolist priest used the little finger of the right hand to touch the brow of the divinity while pronouncing a formula. The main work was now done. The naos, the statue and the sanctuary were sprinkled to return it to a state of purity. Five grains of natron and five grains of another nitrous salt and five grains of resin were presented. The face of the god was veiled and the door was sealed. The final fumigations were made; the morning service was ended.

The midday service was shorter than the dawn opening. It was performed when the sun was at its height. Waters were sprinkled and incense was offered. The evening service was the least solemn of the three. It was in many ways a repetition of the first service except it took place in the side chapel instead. The evening liturgy was chanted. Libations were offered. Finally with the last fumigation the service was finished. The day was over, the god rested.

Daily temple life served to uphold the indwelling presence of the deities. Mystical encounter did not take place in the daily rituals performed by the *wab* priests. It was reserved for those initiated into the mystery heart of the cult. As ever we need to remember the distinction between inner and outer service, between the exoteric and esoteric priesthood. The purified priesthood presented offerings, the initiated priesthood spoke with the gods.

MAGIC HIGH AND LOW.

Among the Parsees, the Medes and the Egyptians, a higher knowledge of nature was understood by the term Magic, with which religion and particularly astronomy were associated. The initiated and their disciples were called Magicians.
A. E. Waite, The Occult Sciences

There is no doubt that Egypt is the fabled home of all things magical. The inexplicable and mysterious always fascinates.

The magical is perceived to be glamorous and powerful. Yet the true heart of Egypt lay in the Mysteries, not in the spell book. The essence of Egyptian tradition is enshrined in Wisdom not in magic. Wisdom and magic are clearly connected. The first is a higher octave of the second. The path of Wisdom seeks to understand the laws of cause and effect so that the individual may take a rightful place in the cosmic scheme. The path of magic seeks to understand the laws of cause and effect so that the individual can manipulate a more comfortable place in the cosmic whole. It is no surprise that we associate Egypt with magic when in fact we should associate it with Wisdom. A Wisdom tradition will always throw up magical by-ways.

All metaphysical traditions seek to discover an underlying reality. This quest must by definition explore the nature of the human being and the workings of the world as part of the cosmos. The Egyptians sought to comprehend the interrelationships between humanity, nature and the cosmos through the careful observation of natural laws. They understood the relationship between cause and effect through a hierarchy of Neters, the divine living powers. The Egyptian tradition was essentially mystical; magic is undoubtedly a component of this path. If we are to understand the relationship between magic and wisdom, we need to see the two as a continuum.

The current priesthood takes a limited view of the acceptable dialogue between the human and the divine and does not seem at all interested in fundamental questions about the human psyche. The Egyptians had a keen interest in the full range of human nature and held a broad view of the dialogue possible between the human and the Neter. In fact certain branches of the priesthood acted as intermediaries between the supplicant and the gods. Oracular prophecy was part of the priestly tradition, it was not a demonized aberration. The higher ranks among the priesthood were called 'prophets' by the Greeks which points to a prophetic function at high levels. Like the State Oracle of Tibet, high level prophecy would have been placed at the service of the pharaoh. We should not expect to find records of such interaction. Public prophecy on the other hand is a matter of record. The oracular ship was a common event processing from five to ten times every month on a well-marked route. The incense bearer walked at the head. The ship halted at various stations where priests performed various fumigations, and here oracles were given out by written consultation. As the oracular ship was carried, any member of the crowd was free to seek personal judgement. The gods spoke through the bearers of the boat who as a single being moved and swayed through the will of the god. As the bearers felt the divine will enter them so the ship appeared to move through its own will. The bearers moved together as a group. Would those at the rear suddenly sink under the insupportable weight? Would the bearers feel themselves being pushed to the front of the ship? Would they lean to one side en masse? Such movements were keenly watched by the crowd and interpreted by the priests; this was the oracle of the ship.

It was also possible to consult the god directly through incubationary sleep undertaken in small chambers within the temple. A story tells that the Lady Mehitouskhet was grieved at her sterility and went to the temple of Imouthes the healer. Here she had a dream. 'One spoke to her, saying; are you not Mehitouskhet, the wife of Satni, who sleeps in the temple to receive a remedy for your sterility through the grace of god? Tomorrow go to the fountain of Satni, your husband, and there you will find a foot of colocase sprouting there. The colocase that you find, you will pull up with its leaves, you will make a remedy from it which you will give to your husband, then you will lie next to him and you will conceive of him this same night.' According to the story she followed the advice and conceived a child as foretold.

At Deir el Medineh we find human everyday questions inscribed on pieces of pottery or limestone. Everyday concerns seem to change little with the passing of time. Will the minister of state give us a new leader now? Have the soldiers stolen? Is one of my goats at the house of Ptahmose? More important matters were also placed before the god. When a priest of Amon was suspected of having stolen from the granaries his case was decided by oracle. Two written statements were presented to the god, and in this instance the priest was found innocent and duly promoted.

It has been said that the Egyptian religion did not include the masses. This is quite false. The supposition is based purely upon our contemporary practice of going to the house of god, the church. Instead the gods went to the people made manifest through the priesthood. The ordinary person was included in the life of the temple through the many festivals, mystery dramas, outings and appearances of the gods who were taken from the dwelling place of the god to the dwelling place of the people by the servants of the god, the hm ntr.

Let us now attempt to share in the unique qualities radiated by the priestesses of Hathor.

THE BEAUTEOUS ONES

Enter your own state of meditation. You stand among a crowd. There is a great festival atmosphere. Everyone is excited. The hot sun beats down upon you. The east bank of the great river is lined with people as far as the eye can see. You know they will be here soon.

A cry goes up. Hands are raised, fingers are pointed. Excited voices rise. Around the bend of the river comes the flotilla. Long boats sweep along, rowed by strong arms in perfect unison. A drumbeat sounds out a rhythm. The flotilla moves as one being. The crowd fall quiet and the drum beat alone sounds out like a heart beat. The flotilla is drawing closer. Now another sound is carried along on the air. Women's voices rise and fall in ripples of sound – their song is like laughter, their chant is the sound of joy.

The flotilla draws closer. Now you hear the rattling of sistrums. The priestesses of Hathor are coming. She is coming. Hathor is coming. Your heart lifts in expectation. The lead boat now approaches. At the centre you see the veiled shrine, and in front of the shrine a small altar stands. Incense rises. The oarsmen rest as the boat glides towards the bank, sistrums rattle and the chanting takes up again. The second and third boats glide into their appointed places. Men from the temple briskly step off and secure the boat to its moorings. Everyone is transfixed by the presence of the boat. All eyes are on it. A woman's solitary voice is raised in invocation, the chief priestess stands before the naos. Two white robed priests offer incense, sistrums rattle. From within the boat a line of priestesses now stand.

Guardians of the shrine step forward. Hathor is unveiled. The Golden One as the nurturing cow is revealed. A note of praise is sounded, sistrums rattle in a crescendo of sound. Her shrine is lifted by the temple bearers. She comes ashore. Everyone makes way for the procession. The Golden One comes, followed by her servants. You recall everything you have heard about these women, truly they are 'the beauteous ones'. They prepare to come among you, to bring Hathor to you, to show you Hathor herself. From the stern of the boat a harpist strikes up a note.

The Hathors are now disembarking, each chanting. The sound seems to light an unknown fire within you. The chants rise and fall and you find yourself following its irresistible rhythm. You want to dance, to move, to respond. Your heart sings within you. The Hathors are coming. You smell their perfume on the breeze. You hear the sound of their anklets tinkling. They draw closer, they approach in a single line moving as one being. They step and sway with a perfect and easy grace which is as indefinable as it is magnetic. You are mesmerized by the dance. They will dance as they follow the Golden One to the temple on the hill. As they dance, the Hathors extend the beaded *menat*. The crowds reach out as if to gather up the invisible blessing of Hathor herself. You remember what you have heard about these women; you want to receive this blessing, to comprehend this beauty, to know this extraordinary, exhilarating power. You are quite near the front of the crowd. They will be coming past soon. The leading Hathor is just in front of you. You want to drink in her features. You want to remember this moment for ever. She is here. The Hathor is here. Her feet and hands are tiny, her limbs have a grace which you cannot comprehend yet you recognize its indefinable presence.

She extends the *menat*. It seems as if this gesture is given just for you. Your eyes meet for just a moment, yet in that moment you have seen the face of Hathor herself. You reach out to Hathor beseeching her to share her divine joy with you. You touch the *menat*. Long life, stability and happiness are bestowed. In that split second something within you awakens to life. You offer thanks to Hathor. You have seen her face through her servants.

You stand in a daze as the procession passes. You hear the sistrums and see the rippling forms passing by as one. You join the procession. You will follow the shrine to the temple on the hill and there you will dance and sing in praise of Hathor and the Beauteous Ones.

4 · The House of the God – Neter Het

Let everyone who enters here be pure.

Temple inscription

If we are to understand the relationship between the institution of the temple and the transmission of its wisdom, we will need to forget any comparison between the ancient temple and the modern church, the current 'God's House'. The temple lay enclosed behind massive walls and huge gates; it was a vast complex of related sanctuaries, chambers, halls and courtyards. Under Rameses III, the temple at Karnak owned 433 gardens, 83 boats, 46 construction yards, 924 square miles of fields, and 65 small market towns. The temple of Amun at Thebes had a staff of more than 81,000 persons. The major temples were fabulously wealthy. Heliopolis owned 170 square miles of land, a staff of 12,963 people and some 45,544 animals. Memphis had a site of 11 square miles and a staff of some 3,000. At the other extreme it was not uncommon for a small sanctuary to have a staff of no more than about twenty persons.

The Egyptian temple was a world set apart. The richer and more powerful temples were like self-contained cities. In this respect at least we can compare an important Egyptian temple to the modern Vatican city, a spiritual power upheld by a vast hierarchical administration of dignitaries, officials and post holders. The organization of temple personnel had all the hallmarks of a contemporary civil service. The everyday upkeep of the huge temple estates lay in the hands of an army of workers of every kind. There were doorkeepers and bakers, offering bearers, artists, engravers, architects and assistants who looked after the animals. In the midst of this army of workers, overseers and administrators, the sacred officiants formed a relatively small number. The exoteric life of the temple was highly structured, efficient and orderly like any large organization. The esoteric life of the temple burned brightly within this body.

The temple was quite simply the dwelling place of the god, the House of Eternity. The complex temple evolved from simple circular reed huts of the predynastic period. In time these sacred dwellings became more elaborate in design and sturdier in construction. Reeds were replaced by unbaked bricks and then by stone. The early form was however retained in the naos, the enclosed shrine which continued to resemble a dwelling with a door.

Egyptian temples were of three main types with quite different functions and traditions. The mortuary temple served the deceased, the cult temple served the god, the solar temple functioned to reflect the primary role accorded to the sun. The mortuary and cult temple originated in the reed shelter. The solar temple evolved into a quite separate tradition centred upon the obelisk. However all temples were modelled upon the story of the first temple; the temple was the architectural embodiment of this sacred story.

THE FIRST STORY

The historical temple in Egypt is regarded as the direct descendant of a primeval temple that was erected on a low mound near the island in which the drama of creation commenced.

E. A. E. Reymond,
The Mythological Foundation of the Egyptian Temple

At the Temple of Horus at Edfu, a set of inscriptions known as the *Building Texts* preserve both the architectural history and symbolic justification. These inscriptions name, describe and explain the function of each part of the temple room by room. The texts include *The Sacred Book of Temples* which presents a list of shrines and sacred places accompanied by their mythological significance. On the inner face of the enclosure wall, we find a group of five texts which probably formed parts of a single book called *Specification of the Mounds of the Early Primeval Age*. We are told that this sacred book was of divine origin, a 'Copy of writings which Thoth made according to the words of the Sages of Mehweret'. The mythological events narrated in the Edfu texts are long and complicated, and no more than a brief résumé is offered here. It was this strange tale and its echoes which established the cult formula by which Egyptian temples were founded.

According to the texts, the first island lay in darkness surrounded by primeval water. Light came and the water grew radiant. Two beings emerged from the water. These deities were called the Two Companions of The Divine Heart, the leaders of the Shebtiw. The two Shebtiw landed upon the island and planted a slip of reed in the primeval water which became a perch. The Sanctified Ruler, in the form of a Divine Falcon, landed. The Shebtiw uttered sacred names – a new domain, the sacred land, came into existence. Thus the story begins.

The tale has all the disorder of a fragmented myth and all the inconsistencies of a long period of accretion. Divine beings appear and create other divine beings, obscure titles abound. Yet we can identify certain themes which were to remain through the millennia. Egypt remained ever faithful to the primeval mound, the island of creation as a sacred image. The word too remained ever powerful. Life appeared through the sacred word. Here we find the familiar *djed* pillar brought into being for the first time by the creator god, Tanen. The many episodes cover the origin of the sacred lands, the homeland of the primeval ones and the characteristics of the sacred site.

At times the text is quite precise. The first temple was established within an enclosure measuring some 300 cubits from west to east and some 400 cubits from north to south. It was established in the presence of Thoth, Lord of Wisdom, Seshat, Lady of Books, the Builder Gods and the Ogdoad, of whom we know nothing. A difference between the temple of the Falcon and a solar temple emerges at a mythological level. The cult of the falcon included funerary associations and acts of revivification to restore the land to a pre-existing sacred nature. The solar temple was associated with other ideas, 'the place for crushing,' where the enemies of the god were killed. The foundation of the sun temple was made in the presence of Re, the Ogdoad, Tanen, a creator god, The Eldest One, the Builder Gods, and the Shebtiw. The Builder Gods were responsible for establishing the enclosure walls. 'The Builder Gods set firmly its four sides', says the Edfu Text. The interior was planned by Thoth and Seshat.

All the ceremonies of founding and consecration which were to be enacted at every new sacred site were recorded here in these early texts. The foundation ceremony of Stretching the Cord was performed here. The text tells us that Thoth spoke: 'I came here in my true form upon the foundation ground of the Great Seat of Harakhte. I caused its long dimensions to be good, its breadth to be exact, all its measurements to be according to the norm, all its sanctuaries to be in the place where they should be and its hall to resemble the sky.' The ceremony of 'Bestowing Names upon the Temple' was recorded here. Finally the 'Festival of Entering' marked the possession of the site by the divinities. These texts may be obscure and at times incomprehensible to us. They were, however, of great importance to the Egyptians. Edfu itself conformed to the mythological temple described in the texts: its enclosure measuerd 300 by 400 cubits.

THE DWELLING PLACE OF THE GOD

The temple is a dynamo, a place of considerable power.
Michael Lundquist, The Temple.

These archetypal themes of the first story were made manifest in stones and symbol, statue and ceremony. Its essence was enshrined in shape and form, structure and layout. Every temple was enclosed within an outer mud brick wall built in sections and alternate convex and concave layers representing the primeval waters. The temple enclosure was reached through a gateway set between great pylons derived from the woven towers which had once guarded the entrance to the reed enclosure. The temple was rectangular in design. One or sometimes two open courtyards were followed by the hypostyle hall, symbolizing the reception area of the deity's residence. Here the columns represented the lush vegetation of the first island. The ceiling represented the sky, and the island plants were carved on the base of the walls. The floor gradually inclined from front to back to reproduce the island of creation. The cult statue was housed at the rear of the temple where provision was also made for the god's possessions, the cult insignia and ritual equipment.

The temple as building was no more than an empty container. It was made sacred through the rituals and ceremonies which were enacted within its walls. The primal act consisted of bringing the temple to life, through a consecration which imbued it with divine life. Themes from the mythological prototype were recreated and elaborated into cult ritual.

Establishing the physical temple began by delimiting the land. The site was founded through the 'Ceremony of Stretching the Cord'. The pharaoh established the boundaries. He drove stakes into the four corners and connected them with a cord. According to the text, 'his hands were on the pole, grasped the cord together with Seshat... to construct its sanctuaries according to the norm'. The ceremony formally established the stellar orientation of the temple. We know that the merkhert, the instrument of knowing, was a part of the ceremony. The pharaoh continued with the founding rituals by 'Setting out the Four Sides of the Enclosure'. All cult acts were fourfold. The first furrow was ploughed four times; the first brick as the primal unification of earth and water was prepared four times; the temple enclosure was purified four times with natron. Once the site was founded, the temple was brought to life through the Festival of Entering. At last in a final ceremony known as Handing over the Temple to its Lord, the temple was initiated into its own life through vivifying the

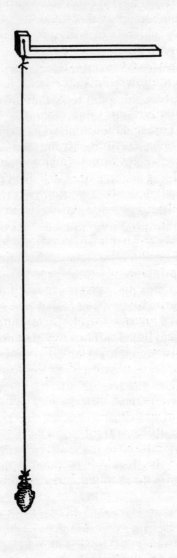

The Merkhert

sacred names. The ceremony was repeated annually and the divine presence was renewed every day by the temple liturgy. The round of ceremonies maintained the divine presence within the temple which in turn maintained the life of Egypt. The Egyptians invited the Neters to inhabit a dwelling as we might invite a guest to stay for an extended visit. The Egyptians invited the gods to indwell indefinitely.

The temple of the god was the god's house; nothing here was random or without meaning. This was a manifestation of Wisdom. The correspondence between the cosmic and the mundane is the language of the Mysteries. It is therefore not surprising that R. A. Schwaller de Lubicz should suggest even the choice of building material used in the temple was a matter of symbolic correspondence. Accordingly stones of igneous origin – diorite, basalt, syenite, black or red granite – were used to represent the principle of fire, obelisks dedicated to Ra for instance. Sandstone being an alluvial deposit symbolized the principle of earth. Limestone, called the white stone, symbolized the principle of air. Unbaked brick formed from Nile mud was called 'the marriage of earth and water' and symbolized the principle of water. The beautiful translucent alabaster was much loved; it carried the meaning of 'becoming' as it originated from limestone in a liquid or muddy state. The most famous alabaster quarry was called *hat-nub*, the house of gold. This phrase also referred to the funerary chamber, another state of becoming. If we are to even touch upon the Egyptian mind-set, we need to prepare ourselves to encounter double meaning at every turn. This is a new departure for us; we are used to a utilitarian not a symbolic use of language. As a student passed through the grades of temple training so a wider symbolic structure was revealed. Symbolic thinking enables mental growth; purely descriptive thinking stultifies mental growth.

The Egyptians were steeped in the symbolic to a degree we cannot comprehend. We come from a society innured to the symbolic. It is no wonder that as Egyptologists insist on a utilitarian explanation, the symbolic resonance is entirely missed. We should place ourselves in symbolic mode if we are to even touch upon the Egyptian mind. The symbol has always been the key to the Mysteries. The symbolic takes many forms; mundane objects, images, colours, shapes, numbers, even architectural forms. This is the first key to the Egyptian Wisdom. Teaching was expressed in symbol, wisdom was revealed through the symbol.

The idea of sacred architecture however should not be entirely foreign to us – the great Cathedral incorporates the cross. The Egyptian temple reveals the human microcosm, according to the Hermetic maxim, As Above So Below. A team led by R. A. Schwaller de Lubicz surveyed the temple at Luxor over a number of years. He concluded that 'the Temple of Luxor is indisputably devoted to the Human Microcosm. This consecration is not merely a simple attribution; the entire temple becomes a book explaining the secret functions of the organs and nerve centres.' In other words he maintained that the temple itself provided esoteric teachings through its implicit architectural and spatial relationships. Moreover he continued 'that what is true for the Temple of Luxor is also true for other monuments from all other Egyptian dynasties, the symbolism evidently having been adapted to the particular consecration of an edifice and to the nature of the place where it was erected'.

We find the Wisdom of the temple not in books but through geometric proportions, symbols, architectural arrangements and mathematical relationships which mean nothing to the uninitiated eye. Here we have a clue in our search for the Wisdom of Egypt. It is blatantly displayed in everything Egyptian. We do not have to look far, we simply have to change the way in which we look for it.

Egypt's reputation for arcane knowledge never fades, yet those who seek this same knowledge mistakenly hope for 'a secret'. There is no single secret, no hidden magical formula, no undiscovered esoteric treatise. Egypt's reputation for arcane mysteries is not unfounded but it has been misrepresented. It is based not on some magical doctrine but on a deep and comprehensive understanding of perfectly natural laws. True magic, theurgy, does not come from the manipulation of natural forces. This produces no more than a dramatic but short-term result, it does not sustain a civilization. Wisdom is founded upon knowledge and flows directly from understanding. Wisdom gives birth to beauty of every kind; it generates harmony through every form. It portrays the inner light through every statement and action. Wisdom shows itself eternally, it can do no other.

THE HOUSE OF LIFE – PER ANKH

I am Isis the great, the god's mother, lady of the House of Life, dwelling in the Beautiful House.
                    Inscription from the coffin of Ankhefenamun

As the exoteric body of the temple was maintained by the hierarchy of administrators, so the esoteric heart of the temple was found within the House of Life. The House of Life remains the most enigmatic of all Egyptian institutions. Its name alone is evocative, typical of the Egyptian mind. The heart of Egyptian Wisdom undoubtedly lies here in this little-understood institution, where the sacred Books of Thoth were kept and studied. Our difficulty lies in the fact that we have no counterpart. It clearly functioned as a library, yet it was more than a library; it functioned as an archive yet it was more than an assembly of historical data. It had connections with magic and ritual, with astronomy and medicine. We cannot reconcile such diverse applications – we see only separation and contradiction where the Egyptians saw unity and harmony. The House of Life was the externalization of the House of Thoth, Lord of Wisdom.

The remains of only one site have been discovered. At El Amarna two small buildings, their bricks individually stamped to read *per ankh*, abut the so-called Records Office, 'The Place of the Correspondence of the Pharaoh'. We know that temples at Memphis, Abydos, Akhmim, Coptos, Esna and Edfu had a House of Life as part of their extensive complex.

The recorded references to the House of Life are surprisingly few down to the reign of Rameses III. Rameses IV, however, expressed a particular interest in all things literary, archaeological and esoteric. According to one inscription, he is described as investigating 'the annals of Thoth who is in the House of Life'. Elsewhere he is described as being 'excellent of understanding like Thoth'. It is said that he 'penetrated into the annals like the maker thereof', having 'examined the writings of the House of Life'. The prince Mentjuhotep is called 'Master of the Secrets of the House of Life'. At El-Bershah, Iha is described as an 'overseer of writings in the House of Life, to whom all private matters are revealed'. A Nineteenth Dynasty tomb at Thebes dating from the reign of Rameses II belongs to Amenwahsu who was described as a 'scribe who wrote the annals of the gods and goddesses in the House of Life.' His son Khaemope carried the same title. He is described as 'one who wrote the annals of all the gods in the House of Life.' Finally he was called, 'divine father of Re-Atum in the House of Life'.

Our sense of mystery deepens. Here is the House of Thoth, the House of Life and the House of Scribes. How can we make sense of this? We are clearly in difficulty: we have no concrete understanding of Wisdom which to us appears to be as insubstantial as candy floss. We are perplexed by an institution which housed both sacred and mundane functions, and are at a loss to comprehend the priestly scribe, the scribal priest. Our very lack of imagination and our spiritual immaturity prevents us from acknowledging the possibility of a holistic spiritual philosophy preserved and transmitted through an institution devoted to its study and learning.

The Egyptians themselves were reticent when it came to speaking about the House of Life. This is hardly surprising. It needed no public justification, it required no acclaim. It worked silently and unobtrusively as befits a holder of the Wisdom tradition. However, the sense of the arcane is never absent. In the Thirtieth Dynasty, Nakhtharab, chief lector priest, is described as 'leader of the masters of magic in the House of Life'. A relief from Bubastis depicting the Sd festival shows a priestly procession described as 'friends and masters of magic'. Two persons are described as 'magician protectors of the king of Lower Egypt'.

We cannot penetrate the secrets of the House of Life, we can only surmise and speculate. Yet we can observe certain realities. We find a balance between the sacred and the mundane which appears disconcerting to us. We have divided the spiritual and the material with such good effect that we find it hard to contemplate how the two jobs were effected by the same individual as priestly scribe and scribal priest. Amenmose was in charge of the grain, yet he also conducted the festivals of Osiris and was head of the stables. Amenwahsu's father, Simut, was a draughtsman but also a scribe. Sacral duties were combined with the everyday activities of accounting and record keeping. Perhaps we might do well to look to the model of the medieval monastery which also combined the spiritual and the material with good effect. The monks too loved learning. Yet we cannot take this analogy too far. The medieval monasteries were created in the service of an exoteric religion, the House of Life served the esoteric Wisdom.

We have relatively few inscriptions which relate to the House of Life. One, however, relates directly to restoration undertaken by the chief physician, Udjehorressnet. He was given the task of restoration by the king. 'His Majesty king Darius commanded me to return to Egypt in order to restore the department(s) of the House(s) of Life . . . after they had fallen into decay. I did as His Majesty commanded me; I furnished them with all their staffs consisting of persons of rank, not a poor man's son among them. I placed them in charge of every learned man (in order to teach them) all their crafts. His Majesty commanded them to be given all (manner) of good things that they might exercise all their crafts. I equipped them with all their ability and their apparatus was on record in accordance with their former condition. This His Majesty did because he knew the virtue of this art to revive all that are sick and to commemorate for ever the name(s) of all the gods, their temples, their offerings and the conduct of their festivals.'

We can only conclude by saying that we undoubtedly find it hard to comprehend Egyptian intent. We have no equivalent contemporary institution and this is surely our loss.

THE OSIRION

Homage to thee, O king of kings, lord of lords, ruler of princes, who from the womb of Nut has ruled the world and the underworld.

Hymn to Osiris

Our brief survey of the Egyptian temple must include the Osirion at Abydos. This structure remains unique in the history of sacred architecture. Abydos was always an important site for the Egyptians. Traditionally it was the burial place of Osiris and also of the royal ancestors. It was a site of pilgrimage long before the Osiris complex was built. The temple site includes a number of buildings both sacred and practical. The Osirion is unique. It was designed as a subterranean hill and included underground water. This unique construction lay directly behind the main temple, which yet again shows us the Egyptian passion for architectural allegory and symbol. It was built for the god of the netherworld and was set in the netherworld. It expressed the process of transformation through death and rebirth as rendered in the myth of Osiris. The Osirion presented the underworld, the realm of the god of the underworld.

In the centre was a platform, the primeval island surrounded by water. Ten large square columns supported the roof. According to Lucy Lamy who has worked extensively on the dimension and proportions of this temple, we find emphasis on $\sqrt{5}$ and $\sqrt{2}$, the numbers of rebirth and self generation. There is no doubt that architecture and idea were one. The Osirion was built as a subterranean house for a subterranean god. This idea is confirmed by the Egyptologist Rosalie David who says that 'the temple and the Osirion were designed to form a unit, both architecturally and mythologically'. She also says that 'the ritual within this unique complex was obviously connected with the death and resurrection of Osiris and the identification of Sethos with Osiris and his ultimate resurrection as King of the Dead. The rite of raising the Djed Pillars symbolized this rebirth and ensured the renewal of the powers of Osiris.' The unique purpose of the Osirion has been debated. If it is purely the burial place of a single pharaoh who chose the Osiris myth for his personal memorial, it is curious that of all the many Egyptian kings, each identified as Osiris risen, Sethos alone chose to preserve this identity in stone. It is more in keeping with the Mystery tradition that it was here that the inner priesthood of Osiris were initiated through a literal descent into the netherworld.

Let us now journey in the mind to the Egyptian temple. If we are blessed we may receive a revelation.

THE HOUSE OF ETERNITY

Enter your own state of meditation. You are invited into the God's House as a special and honoured guest. You stand before the great pylon wall wondering what lies beyond. It is very early in the morning. Dawn is just breaking and the air is already warm. The huge gates are closed – flags flutter from flag poles. Dawn rises. You hear the sound of a great wooden bar being drawn. The doors part and then swing open. The doorkeepers finish their task and fasten back the doors. You are free to enter. You are in a courtyard. From inside, the courtyard seems even bigger than you had expected. You walk across to the enclosure wall to have a better look at the construction. You find that the courses are laid convex upon concave. It produces a wave-like effect and you are reminded of rippling water.

Your attention is drawn away as a group of linen-clad young men appear. They approach and beckon for you to follow; you feel welcomed and join their group. You walk in silence. Soon you stand before the waters of the sacred lake. Each man waits in turn to descend the steps into the waters. Each completes the first ablution of the day accompanied by set prayers. You await a turn and step into the waters. You ask for a blessing on your inner journey. The temple seems to be coming to life around you. You hear voices in the distance. A group of offering bearers, trays held high, cross the courtyard. The young priests have gone about their business, you stand alone beside the lake.

A single figure now walks towards you. He greets you and explains that he will be your guide. He turns and you follow until you stand together in the first hall. Here, great columns support a high ceiling. Wherever you look you see brilliant colour. The columns are carved and painted with figures and signs that you do not understand. Nevertheless their beauty speaks directly to you. The ceiling, too, is decorated using every imaginable colour. You want to ask what everything

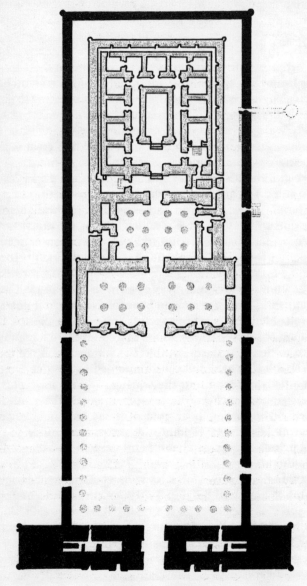

Plan of a Temple

means but you know there is so much to ask about. As you wander through the hall, small groups of priests pass by. A figure approaches; your guide makes a deep and respectful obeisance as he passes, no words are spoken. The air here is filled with the delightful scents of aromatic incense. The hall is a place of both beauty and delicacy.

You sense that it is time to move on and follow your guide. At the far end of the hall is a door. You look beyond the doorway. The light is dim and shafts of sunlight pierce the darkness laying down patterns on the stone floor. Your guide passes through and you follow. There are columns here too but their brightness is withheld. The place is quite silent – you feel that you too wish to enter into an inner silence of your own. You notice your guide seems to have withdrawn into private meditation. The darkness and the tranquillity bequeaths its own inner state.

Your guide walks on. You pass through another door at the far end of the hall. You know that you have been permitted to enter into the sacred domains where the god dwells. You follow your guide. A new feeling comes over you. You realize that in this place only thoughts of adoration are generated. There is something sacred in this atmosphere. In the centre of the hall is the enclosed sanctuary where the god dwells. You hear a voice from within the chamber and realize that your visit has coincided with the morning service; you hear a chanted refrain and smell burning incense on the air. You know that you will not be permitted to enter the most holy shrine and gaze upon the face of the divinity. The pharaoh alone, in person or through his representative the high priest, adores the god. Yet you have been permitted to come this far – you stand on sanctified ground. If you wish, address the divinity from your heart. Speak your word in silence but speak in truth, for Maat is always offered before the gods. Your guide will wait.

When you are ready to depart, realize that you tread the processional way around the inner sanctuary. As you walk past the doors to the chapels you see that every wall, every door lintel and jamb is covered in signs, beautifully portrayed. You pass by a number of doors. At each one your guide stops and announces its name to you. The very titles stir your imagination. You complete a circuit around the sanctuary and find yourself back at the doorway between the halls. Looking far ahead you see a square of brilliant light. You realize that all the doorways within the temple are directly aligned. The light draws you on; you pass through both halls and find yourself outside again in the open courtyard. You feel you have returned from another place. Your guide escorts you to the gateway in the pylon wall. Make your thanks and complete your return to full waking consciousness.

5 · THE SACRED SCRIPT – THE MEDU NETERS

> In order to conform to the true meaning of the symbol
> in ancient Egypt, we should use the term Medu Neter,
> the Egyptian meaning of which is distorted by the Greek
> translation hieroglyph. The Medu Neters are the Neters or
> principles – conveyed by a sign.
>
> Isha Schwaller de Lubicz, Her-Bak, Egyptian Initiate

The Ancient Egyptians were among the earliest people to
produce a written language. Hieroglyphs originated in the
late predynastic period and remained in use until 394 AD,
a period of some 4,000 years. This sacred language was
remarkably unchanged by time. The necessary impetus for
change produced mundane variations, hieratic and demotic.
Hieroglyphic script was preserved as the sacred language.

The Greeks called the individual elements of the Egyptian
script *ta hiera grammat*, 'the sacred letters', or *ta hieriglyphica*,
'the sacred carved letters', from which our term hieroglyphics is derived. The Egyptians themselves referred to their
hieroglyphic signs as *Medu Neter*, 'the signs of the gods'.
Once again the Greek translation falls short of the original
intent. The individual hieroglyph was called a 'sign', 'image'
or 'form'. The aesthetics of the script were always important,

conventions developed to harmonize presentation and layout. Hieroglyphic script employs a balance between the sign as sound and the sign as idea. It was this balance between the phonic and the pictorial which kept potential translators confused for so long. A further class of sign functioned as a determinative, indicating the exact meaning of a word.

With the final breakdown of the Egyptian civilization, hieroglyphics passed from reality to memory. When travellers rediscovered Egypt, the strange and beautiful script was a complete mystery. Several hopeful translators tried their luck but with only limited success. However in 1799 a commemorative stone was found bearing an inscription dated from year 9 in the reign of Ptolomy V Epiphanes recording the honours bestowed on the temple by the king. We know this as the Rosetta Stone. This single discovery opened the door to the Egyptian script. The Rosetta Stone was a translator's dream bearing three different scripts; hieroglyphic, demotic and Greek.

We are used to a language based purely upon a phonic code, so we will first look at the Medu Neters in this context.

THE HIEROGLYPHIC ALPHABET

Translit.	Sign
a	
i	
y	
ʿ	
w	
b	
p	
f	

Translit.	Sign

m	
n	
r	
h	
ḥ	
ḫ	
ẖ	
s	
ś	
š	
ḳ	
k	
g	
t	
ṯ	
d	
ḏ	

73

Additionally there were a number of signs that served as biconsonant groups.

Sign	Transliteration	Sign	Transliteration
	pr		*nb*
	hr		*ss*
	wp		*ns*
	mn		*hh*
	mr		
	ms		*tt*

Finally a third group served as triconsonant groupings.

Sign	Transliteration	Sign	Transliteration
	nfr		*kh pr*
	ntr		*djd*
	hrw		*tbn*
	htp		*nhm*

We can relate to the mundane needs of a complex society. We understand record keeping and list making, categorizing and calculating. Egyptian society was well ordered, meticulous accounts were kept of everything: taxes, population census, calculations for building projects and the everyday work of temple administration. We can appreciate this, the mundane use of the written word. In the first century BC Diodorus tells us that 'the priests teach their sons two kinds of writing; that which is called sacred and that which is more widely used for instruction'. This is the single most important key to the purpose and nature of what we have come to call hieroglyphic writing, the Medu Neters. Its nature was dual, its purpose was dual, the sacred and the mundane were blended most perfectly as exoteric and esoteric script.

THE EXOTERIC SCRIPT

In order to understand the profane–exoteric meaning of the hieroglyphic texts, the grammar of Egyptology is sufficient.
Isha Schwaller de Lubicz, Her-Bak, Egyptian Initiate

In Egypt the status of the scribe was remarkably high. Important scribes had their own tombs. Taxation, accounting, local organization, record keeping, temple inventories, all were in the hands of the scribes. Egypt needed scribes. As demands for a highly trained bureaucracy intensified, scribal training moved from an informal apprentice system to the palace school. In the New Kingdom, open air classes were held at the mortuary temple of Rameses II at Thebes, the temple of Mut at Karnak and at the temple of Amun.

Scribes first learned to write on ostraca, limestone flakes and potsherd, the cheapest material available. They were first taught to copy, later they wrote from dictation and eventually from memory. Scribes were also expected to train the memory through learning long lists which were collectively called 'onomastica'. This is a typical example. 'Here begins the teaching, in order to expand the mind, to teach the ignorant, to know everything that is: what Ptah created, what Thoth brought into being, the sky and the objects on the earth, and what is in it, what mountains spew forth, what Nun covers, all things on which Re shines, everything that grows on the back of the earth, conceived by Amenope, scribe of the holy books in the House of Life.' At its most mundane the scribal profession produced competent record keepers. At its most sublime it produced men of great learning and wisdom. Scribes were expressly trained through a unique Egyptian literary form, the Wisdom literature.

THE WISDOM LITERATURE

You are a man who listens to words so as to distinguish good from bad. Pay attention and listen to my speech; do not neglect what I have said.

The Teaching of Amennakhte

The Wisdom Literature consisted of moral precept and edifying instruction. Such instructions were originally written from a father to son, though this form may well have accorded with a practice of referring to pupils as 'sons' and 'children'. The scribal curriculum was designed both to teach writing skills and also to establish a scribal ethos. The following interaction preserves a moment in this developing process. 'You have come equipped with great mysteries. You tell me a saying of Hardjedef, but do not know whether it is good or bad. Which chapter preceded it? What follows it? You are, of course, a skilled scribe at the head of his fellows, and the teaching of every book is incised on your mind.' The words of Hardjedef have been pieced together though his original work has been lost. Another scribal primer, that of Kagemni, has also been partially preserved. Imhotep, the archetypal scribe and sage, was the author of another work which has sadly been lost to us. The *Instructions of Ptahhotep* alone remains.

THE INSTRUCTIONS OF PTAHHOTEP

The instruction of the superintendent of the capital, the vizier Ptahhotep, under his majesty of King Isesi, who lives for ever and ever.

Do not be arrogant because of your knowledge, and have no confidence in that you are a learned man. Take counsel with the ignorant as with the wise, for the limits of excellence cannot be reached, and no artist fully possesses his skill. A good discourse is more hidden than the precious green stone, and yet it is found with slave-girls over the mill stones.

If you are a leader and give commands to the multitude, strive after every excellence, until there is no fault in your nature. Truth is good and its worth is lasting, and it has not been disturbed since the day of its creator; whereas he that transgresses its ordinance is punished. It lies as a (right) path in front of him that knows nothing. Wrong-doing (?) has never brought its venture to port. Evil indeed wins wealth, but the strength of truth is that it endures, and the (upright) man says: 'It is the property of my father.'

If you are one that sits where stands the table of one who is greater than you, take, when he gives, that which is set before you. Look not at that which lies before him, but look at that which lies before you. Do not shoot many glances at him, for it is an abhorrence to the Ka if one offends it. Cast down your countenance until he greets you, and speak only when he has greeted you. Laugh when he laughs – that will be pleasing in his heart and what you do will be acceptable.

If you are a humble person and in the train of a man of repute, one that stands well with the god, know nothing of his former insignificance. Do not raise your heart against him on account of what you know about him aforetime. Reverence him in accordance with what has happened to him, for wealth does not come of itself . . . It is god that creates repute.

If you are one to whom petition is made, be kind when you hear the speech of the petitioner. Do not deal roughly with him. A petitioner is well pleased if one nods his address until he has made an end of that about which he came.

If you desire your conduct to be good, to set yourself free from all that is evil, then beware of covetousness, which is a malady, diseaseful, incurable. Intimacy with it is impossible; it makes the sweet friend bitter, it alienates the trusted one from the master, it makes bad both father and mother, and it divorces a man's wife.

THE ESOTERIC SCRIPT

There is no difference, as a matter fact, between the texts called hieroglyphs and most of the precepts of Pythagoras.

Plutarch

Every temple had its library and archive. Papyrus scrolls included the subject of myth, religious rituals, medicine, geometry, astronomy and the law. The senior scribes were no doubt immersed continuously in every branch of learning, for all branches of learning were represented in the Sacred Wisdom. Imhotep was the scribal ideal. He embodied the practical application of wisdom. As an architect he applied practical knowledge, as High Priest he served Sacred Wisdom. He became chancellor and was deified as the son of Ptah. Here was the best that scribal training produced. We should be reminded too of Pythagoras who emerged from Egypt with a holistic philosophy. In the temple, astronomy and architecture, medicine and magic, duty and divinity were inseparable one from the other.

The higher ranking scribes were attached to the House of Life as part of the priesthood. If we examine the titles accorded here, we find a clear hint of the arcane. The prince Mentjuhotep is called 'Master of the Secrets of the House of Life'. Iha is described as an 'overseer of writings in the House of Life, to whom all private matters are revealed'. The astronomer priest, Harkhebi, is described as being 'wise in the sacred writings'. If we are only able to comprehend the mundane application of writing, we will have missed the most vital presentation of Wisdom itself, the Medu Neter.

The scribal arts of writing, medicine and magic were under the aegis of Thoth, Lord of Wisdom, who is said to have established a common tongue, invented letters and named objects, given the first principles of music and the basis of astronomy. Thoth is depicted with the head of an ibis and carries the scribal palette or the roll papyrus. He is often shown in the act of using the brush exactly like a scribe. The written word and all the possibilities that a written language brings for encoding and transmitting knowledge are but a part of the gift of Thoth. The Medu Neters are the gift of Thoth. All scribes, regardless of status, were described as the servants of Thoth. In Egypt the relationship between any divinity and the serving priesthood was a dynamic one. The divinity provided a model, the priesthood lived out the cult values, and also sought to embody the nature of the presiding god or goddess. The Egyptian Thoth was the fountainhead of a Wisdom tradition which passed far beyond Egypt, moving through Greek hands as Hermetic philosophy. The Thrice-Great Hermes, Hermes Trismegistus, is Thoth, Lord of Wisdom. Schwaller de Lubicz reminds us that 'the science of Thoth is the sacerdotal science of all times'. The Wisdom of Egypt was the Wisdom of Thoth.

We are in truth mesmerized by this unique and beautiful means of writing. There is a deep fascination in these exotic images. As we gaze at these unfamiliar signs, we suspect that something eludes our minds, and, of course, we are absolutely right. The Egyptians loved a puzzle, an enigma. They delighted in word play and loved to immerse symbol within symbol, to encode meaning in sign, image and form. Plutarch recognized this fact. 'Through symbols ... they reveal certain images of mystical ideas that are hidden and invisible.' Plotinus too recognized that the hieroglyphic script was a means of transmitting the esoteric idea. He wrote 'the sages of Egypt appear to have a consummate knowledge or a marvellous instinct when, in order to reveal their wisdom to us, they did not resort to letters to express words and statements representing sounds but expressed and portrayed objects by "hieroglyphics" and in their mysteries symbolically assigned an emblem of its own to each of them.'

The Egyptians were obsessed with the word, it was the instrument of creation. The expression of the divine word could not be changed but only preserved. It had to pass in original form from generation to generation. The driving impetus in this priesthood was to maintain the status quo. Change was inimical, the transmission of divine order was all important. In the novel *Her-Bak, Egyptian Initiate*, the fictionalized sage speaks: 'certain men great in true science came to organize our country in heaven's image that wisdom might be preserved and cultivated here in a "sealed jar". They set going the system best suited for its transmission, which could only have come about because of the pre-existence of a philosophical tradition and because at the outset exact thinking co-ordinated all its elements, existing and to come.'

SACRED REALITIES

*Each hieroglyph is therefore in itself the living symbol of the
meaning sought.*
            Isha Schwaller de Lubicz, Her-Bak, Egyptian Initiate

Every hieroglyph requires a key if we are to grasp its full
significance. As further levels of meaning and subtlety become
apparent, it is difficult to conceal our sense of admiration at
the skill of their originators. Here is a sacred language par
excellence. For instance, the name of the god Ptah was written
using the phonetic values; 'p' represented by the sky, 't' as the
earth, and 'h' as the figure of a god with raised arms. According
to the Memphite theology, Ptah separated the heaven and the
earth.

In putting the figure of the god between the sky and the
earth, his name revealed his creative function.

The world of the dead, the *duat*, is spelt 'd', plus 't'. These are
also the sounds used to spell the word 'body' and 'eternity'.
The hieroglyph for the Duat shows the serpent curled around
a prone mummy. Thus a simple word serves to both spell out
its name but also reveal its nature. Here two tiny images evoke
body, underworld guardian and eternity.

Neith, an ancient primordial goddess, was represented by 'n',
a vulture and 't', the sun, a simple enough combination.
However each of these two signs has other meanings. More
often the vulture signified mother, *mwt*. The sun signified the
sun god Ra. These two signs together spell the name of Neith,
yet together they point out her relationship as mother of Ra.
The vulture was itself an important and powerful symbol
in Egypt. It was the queen who wore the vulture crown in
her cultic identification with the mother goddess Mut, wife
of Amen-Ra the sun god. The logical mind begins to reel.

Language as evocation is immensely powerful. Word play is not finished; Neith can also be written by spelling the 't' with the sign for land, *ta*, in combination with the sign for water, 'n'. This particular hieroglyph represents ruffled water. By spelling the same name in a different way, we are presented with a different set of ideas. Here is Neith as 'the primeval water which gave birth to the land,' a theologically familiar concept. Once again a brief word encapsulates both divine name and divine function.

Schwaller de Lubicz reminds us repeatedly that we do need to look for a convoluted symbolism. The Medu Neters were chosen in such a way as to really signify all the qualities and functions implicit in the image. We are of course removed from the direct observation of vulture and ibis, crocodile and falcon. It is hard for us to understand the subtleties of movement, habit or life cycle which prompted a recognition deep in the Egyptian mind. It is well known that the humble dung beetle was raised to a sacred status from its simple egg-laying habit. The young emerged from the ball of dung as new life unbegotten. It is less well known that the scarab resembles the human skull, its two wing cases being reminiscent of the two halves of the human skull.

The ability to find the cosmic in the mundane through a correspondence is the hallmark of a mind sensitized through symbolic training. Any contemporary Qabalist recognizes this function for what it is, the inner workings of an esoteric system. These brief examples serve to illustrate the workings of both the Egyptian mind and the Egyptian tradition. Each letter had its own secret; all sacred alphabets are constructed in this way. Moreover a sacred language always serves a double purpose, a written double entendre. To the uninitiated there is no secret to hide. The language functions perfectly well at a purely practical level. To the initiated there exists another level of inner meaning as opposed to the apparent meaning. The inner meaning requires no elaborate subterfuge. It is there all the time, open and blatant. It is hidden from view only because it represents a higher non-cerebral consciousness which simply evades the logical mind.

The Egyptians preserved this double function with astonishing brilliance and clarity over an immensely long period of time. Hebrew still functions as a sacred alphabet. Each of its letters signifies ideas, numbers and cosmic principles. A word becomes a code for an abstraction, a metaphysical concept, an esoteric teaching. An outsider cannot penetrate into the labyrinthine maze of meanings without becoming lost in ideas and distracted by elusive possibilities. A guide is always required in such matters – scribal training took place through an apprenticeship system. It is a mistake to think that we might uncover how the scribes viewed individual hieroglyphs by simply applying any meaning that springs to our mind. It is clear that individual signs and arrangements carried a precise range of corresponding symbols.

Isha Schwaller de Lubicz acts as our guide into the intricacies of an individual hieroglyph in the book *Her-Bak*.

The letter r is written in the lenticular shape of a half open mouth. Now look for the ideas, qualities and functions this sign represents. First, its nature. The mouth, *ra*, is the upper opening of the body, an entrance that communicates by two channels with the lungs and stomach; that is why this hieroglyph is also the generic word for an entrance, *ra*. The mouth opens and shuts to eat, breathe and speak, as the eye, *ar.t*, opens and shuts to receive or refuse light. The mouth's function is dual, passive and active, it receives air and food, emits breath and voice. The eye's function is dual, likewise the reception of light and expression of organic and emotional response. The mouth's shape changes by the separation of the lips for the performance of its function. Opening, it widens or narrows like the shadow thrown on a disc by another disc which gradually eclipses it. In the partially occulted disc, the lentil or dark mouth is the complement of the crescent still visible. This gradual change of shape produces portions of different size that represents parts of the occulted disc. The characteristic has given the name *ra* to parts of a whole such as numerical fractions, chapters and so forth.

These profound thoughts revolve around a single letter. What majestic insights might we discover if only someone would serve as our guide through all the hieroglyphic combinations! Here is a way of thinking quite unlike our own, a mind-set far removed from our utilitarian use of language. This totally symbolic thinking produced completely practical applications, as we see through Egypt's many lasting achievements. There are no grounds whatsoever for thinking that this symbolic system produced woolly mindedness. On the contrary it gave rise to a mind that was both extensive and focused, deep and creative, traditional yet original.

MYTHS AND MYSTERIES

We must not treat the myths as wholly factual accounts, but take what is fitting in each episode according to the principle of likeness (to truth).

Plutarch, de Isis et Osiride

It is abundantly clear that the Egyptians had a deep interest in the cosmos. Thoth himself, the guardian of Sacred Wisdom, bestowed the principles of astronomy. We have already seen how the Egyptians embedded astronomical fact in myth and personified cosmic event and reality. The several cosmic cycles are relationships of time and movement. Such relationships can also be expressed mathematically through number. Scholars involved in the study of ancient myths have long been aware that certain numbers recur in the stories of disparate cultures and times. Let us examine the myth of Osiris in the light of the numbers that we find expressed in it. Jane Sellers has already made this connection for us.

The phenomena of Precession has the effect of causing the stars to appear to have pulled eastwards, that is back below the horizon, at an observed rate along the ecliptic of approximately 50 seconds of arc per year. It is this measurement that directly determines the computation of the total time necessary for the zodiacal constellation to return to its place as a marker of the spring equinox. In 72 years, 50 seconds a year amounts to approximately 1 degree. Then, if one has divided up the circle into 12 equal parts, and each of those into 30 parts or degrees, one has a circle with 360 parts.

$360 \times 72 = 25,920$, that is, the number of years in the Great Year.

It is well known that Plutarch was far more than a disinterested recorder. He was himself a priest and he understood the Egyptian mind very well. He wrote: 'there is nothing more characteristic of Pythagorean philosophy than the use of symbols, such as those employed in the celebration of the mysteries. It is a language. What is said is very clear and obvious to those who are used to this language; it is obscure and unintelligible only to the uninformed. The apparent meaning of these symbols is not the true one, but in it one must search for what they seem to conceal.' Plutarch took it upon himself to present a coherent account of Isis and Osiris. He opens his account with the story of the creation of the epagonemal days, thus providing an astronomical setting. He states that Osiris is the offspring of Cronos, that is time. He specifically mentions the number of days in the original Egyptian year, 360. This is described as being 12 months of 30 days each. Osiris leaves Egypt. Set, along with 72 companions, plans the murder. Set has secretly obtained the 'measure' of Osiris. Nowhere in the original texts do we find the number 72. Plutarch may well have incorporated an element from an oral teaching.

$72 \times 30 = 2,160$, that is, the number of years required for one shift through a complete sign of the zodiac,

$2,160 \times 12 = 25,920$, the number of the Great Year

$72 \times 360 = 25,920$

Let Jane Sellers have the last word. 'Plutarch has given the exact value needed to calculate the number of years for one 30° segment to be replaced with another and, furthermore, the figures needed to obtain the number of years in a Great Year.'

The Medu Neters can still speak to us. Eternal truths do not fade but await rediscovery. There can be no doubt that it was the Egyptian delight to encode the cosmic in the mundane; let us attempt to share that delight as we marvel at the extraordinary language known to the world as hieroglyphs but known to its initiates as 'the signs of the gods'. Let us journey in the mind to the temple, the source of all Wisdom

THE MASTER OF THE MEDU NETERS

Enter a state of meditation. Your imagination has become fired by the Medu Neters. You would genuinely like to know more. You must travel to the temple to find someone who will help you. Formulate your desire for genuine knowledge. All students of the Sacred Wisdom have a deep inner need for learning. For such souls, knowledge is as nourishing as food.

Find yourself seated upon papyrus matting in an empty chamber. The walls are quite devoid of decoration. To one side there is a door. Slits high up in the walls admit shafts of light. The door opens. A young man comes in and sits upon the same matting directly opposite you. He carries something under his arm wrapped in a white cloth. His face has an extraordinary clarity. 'Your thoughts have brought you here,' he says. 'I can show you very little in so short a time. Yet your visit shall be worthwhile.'

He draws out an intricately carved item from beneath the white cloth and places it on the matting between you. It is very beautiful; you recognize the translucent beauty of alabaster. 'What do you see?' You answer and in truth you see an object of great beauty. 'Look beyond appearance.' He points and you now see that two *ankhs* with hands hold *was* sceptres. 'The *ankh*, the Key of Life, shows us spirit and matter in balance. The *ankh* holds the Key of the Nile, the staff cut from the branch when the sap is rising. Its Sethian head reminds us that duality arises from creation. See the sedge of Upper Egypt and the papyrus of Lower Egypt, the twin heraldic devices of the Two Lands. The papyrus is a natural symbol of life itself, its green flush was used to portray concepts such as "joy" and "youth" and "to flourish". The papyrus was connected with Hathor who holds a papyrus staff. See the goddess Hathor upon the vase. She is the goddess of joyful life. She also receives the dead. The water lily, the lotus, closes at night, sinking underwater to reappear the next day. It symbolizes the daily reappearance of the sun and continuous creation. The lotus symbolizes immortality. *The Book of Coming Forth by Day* contains the spell for "transforming oneself into a lotus", that is attaining the resurrected life. See how lotus images are used to ornament the border of the vase. The vase itself is formed in the shape of the *sma* sign which signifies union; most often it represents the union of the Two Lands. It is signified by the heart and the trachea which are inseparable. See the *renpet*, the notched palm branch, the measure of time. It implies "length of time" and "year". Such branches were probably presented to the king at accession and at the *hb sed* festival. The palm branch was the symbol of the god Heh, the personification of eternity. It was found in the hands of three deities shown in the *Book of What is in the Underworld*; The Opener of Time, the Carrier and The Guardian of Time. The *renpet* is connected with the goddess Seshat, She who reckoneth the life-period, Lady of Years, Lady of Fate. It is said that "she notches or carves the years of the life-period". See the name of the owner is written here too within the royal cartouche. See the nomen, Son of Re, Tutankhamun, *heqa-Iuna-shema*, living-image-of-Amun, ruler of Upper-Egyptian-Heliopolis. See the prenomen, *nebkheprure*, the Lordly manifestation of Re.

Remember too that what you see is carved from alabaster which reminds us of a state of becoming. The finest quality comes from but one quarry, the house of gold, *hat nub*. The royal burial chamber is also called the "house of gold" and it too is a place of becoming.'

He covers the beautiful object with the cloth again and you realize that it is almost time to leave. You have been inspired by what you have understood in such a brief moment of time. Before you leave you ask a question. 'Can you say anything that will help me in my researches?' He replies, 'The cardinal rule is this. Think simply, eschew criticism and specious arguments and go straight to the natural fact that a symbol exhibits. Then having closely examined it in all its aspects you will discern the universal law which the natural fact symbolizes. Never neglect the image or form of a hieroglyph whether it is a representation of a thing or animal, or as mythical composition such as the animal Set or Anubis; it is made up of natural constituents every detail of which has a symbolic meaning.'

He leaves the room. You say your thanks and, holding all that you have understood within you, close the meditation.

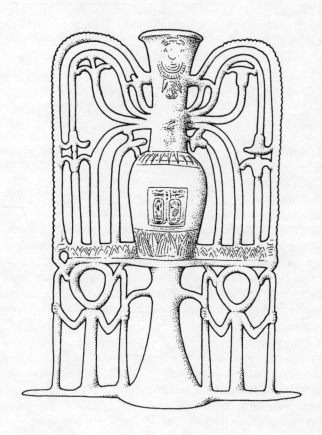

6 · THE RITES OF STATE – NETEM

There is a very common form of reference to the king which indicated that a god was embodied in the physical frame of the pharaoh.

Henri Frankfort, Kingship and the Gods

If we are to truly understand the Egyptian civilization, we have to wrestle with the Egyptian concept of kingship. We cannot simply project our contemporary notions of monarchical rule onto the person of the pharaoh. There is no comparison. We cannot understand the Wisdom of the temple nor the function of the priesthood without reference to the institution of kingship. The pharaoh, the great house, was the high priest to the nation.

The word *hm* is usually translated as 'majesty' which is the only modern term that we have to offer in this context. However the term originally meant 'body' or 'physical appearance'. The date formulas are usually rendered as 'under the majesty of King N' or 'in the lifetime of the majesty of the King N', but more properly translate as 'during the incarnation of King N' or 'during the lifetime of the embodiment of King N'. This usage expressly shows that, in the words of Frankfort, 'the earthly ruler incorporates an immortal god'.

To the Egyptians, the divinity of the pharaoh was no mere idea but an assured and incontrovertible reality. Our understanding of kingship in no way prepares us to accept the literal divinity of the king as understood by the Egyptians. The historian Frankfort recognized this: 'Horus, perpetually reincarnated in successive pharaohs'. This startling claim is our starting point for comprehending the institution of kingship, the civilization of Egypt and the Wisdom of the temple, for it was through the temple that the man-king became the Horus-king.

The pharaoh bore five names which covered his extended identity. He carried the Horus name, followed by a personal epithet which defined the particular Horus incarnation, the Nebty title which referred to the dual monarchy of north and south, the 'Horus of Gold' name which represented the perfected Horus, the dynastic title, 'He of the Sedge and the Bee', and finally he was named the 'Son of Re', the solar principle incarnate.

This god-king played a vital part in the life of the nation in a way that we cannot comprehend. The state ceremonials are of great significance not just as political rites but as esoteric enactment. They are the very empowering rites through which Horian power descended upon the being of the pharaoh.

Egyptian kingship emerged at the end of the predynastic period. Narmer was the first legendary king, Menes unified Egypt. The unified Egypt was revolutionary in concept – it demanded a new theology. The Memphite Theology was born. The emergence of the First Dynasty and the political unification which it brought reconciled oppositions deep in the Egyptian psyche. Menes founded a new capital called The White Walls. This was later to be named Memphis. He reconciled the White Crown of Upper Egypt and the Red Crown of Lower Egypt. The heraldic plants, the sedge of Upper Egypt and the papyrus of Lower Egypt, were placed at the entrance to the temple in the new capital. It symbolized a union that was to last some thirty dynasties.

This philosophical justification placed kingship in a cosmological setting. The role of the pharaoh was inextricably bound to the life of the gods, most especially to Horus and Osiris. The period of disunity which preceded unification, symbolized as the conflict between Horus and Set, was reconciled mythologically when Geb, god of the earth, assigned the whole country to Horus as the rightful heir to his father's throne. The legitimate heir was declared to be Horus, the avenger of his father Osiris. The pharaoh became the living Horus and the deceased Osiris. He held rightful rulership in both kingdoms. As a further affirmation of the rightful lineage, Memphis was described as the burial place of Osiris. The new capital was therefore mythologically justified. The god and the new capital were jointly justified.

RITES OF SUCCESSION

The Egyptians conceived kingship as an institution involving two generations.

Henri Frankfort, Kingship and The Gods

The Egyptians viewed kingship as an integral part of the divinely ordered universe. A royal death created a tear in the cosmic fabric – it was a dangerous break in divine order. The society of men and gods had to be instantly knit together. The answer was to appoint the son as co-regent so that on the death of the king, the co-regent would rule straight away. Succession had to be a smooth transition of power, a seamless transfer of authority through two stages of accession and coronation. The prince took up the crown on the day following a royal death. At dawn the new pharaoh ascended to the throne of his father by actualizing the mythic deed of the sun god, father of all pharaohs who climbed the primeval hill causing the day to break. The same verb was used to express the rising of the sun and the ascending of the throne. The sun was held to be the primal creative power. It had emerged from the primeval ocean. Its regular course also suggested victory, order, immortality and countless rebirths to the Egyptian mind.

King Tutmosis III went up to heaven;
He was united with the sun disc;
The body of the god joined who had made him.
When the next morning dawned
The sun disc shone forth,
The sky became bright,
King Amenhotep II was installed on the throne of his father.

The titulary was drawn up in the House of Life and given to the officials throughout the land. While the deceased king withdrew, the new king, already appointed, prepared to take up the reigns of kingship through the two phases of accession and coronation. His accession to the throne secured continuity. The actual coronation waited on the moment of cosmic harmony. Power was finally transferred at the coronation which was always delayed until an appropriate cosmic tide such as New Year's Day, the equinox or solstice points. It was quite often held over to the first day of the first month Tybi, the Season of Coming Forth. Meanwhile the body of the late king was prepared for burial. During the period between accession and coronation, the new king travelled throughout the land. He visited the main shrines, performing the Mystery Play of the Succession at the significant towns.

THE MYSTERY PLAY OF THE SUCCESSION

It is a view alien to our way of thinking that a ceremony should be not a token act, but an act which changes actuality.
Henri Frankfort, Kingship and the Gods

During this period before the actual coronation, the king enacted the ritualized transfer of power. Although we refer to this drama as a play, this falls far short of the Egyptian intention. Dramatic enactment was never profane but always sacred. It was the mediating vehicle through which the gods were made present. Here was the mystery of succession through which the Horian power was transferred from the dead to the living. It was not a play.

We are fortunate to have what is in effect the script of the actual drama performed at his accession. We have the coronation document from the reign of Sesostris I, who was the second king of the twelfth dynasty. It presents an extraordinary insight into the relationship between the pharaoh and the gods. This mystery calls upon royal princes, officials, priests and craftsmen. It consists of forty-six scenes which can be categorized into six successive parts.

Part 1. (scenes 1–7) The preparation of the accessories, the royal barge and the barge of the royal princes – various sacrifices are made.

Part 2. (scene 8) The royal insignia and mace are brought out of the hall which was also used in the sd festival – the presentation of the insignia is accompanied by references to Horus as rightful heir. The last stage direction at this point says 'marching to the mountains'. It is possible at this point that the king had to make a processional march beyond the town up to the edge of the desert cliffs, to establish dominion over the valley.

Part 3. (scenes 9–18) Further preparations of barges, participants and sites. Barley is threshed by driving bulls and male asses over it, bread made from it will be eaten later. Trees and branches are bought onto the royal barge. Libation is made over the heads of animals – this is intended as a sacrifice to the god of the locality where the play is being performed. The djed pillar is erected at the sites thus consecrated; after the djed pillar is let down again, the royal princes mount their barges. A mock battle is fought, symbolizing the discord which his accession brings to an end – the arbiter is Geb.

Part 4. (scenes 19–25) The produce of the land is brought to the king, the produce of fields and mines is displayed. Milkmaids, butchers, cabinet makers are brought before the king in pairs. This section culminates in a meal.

Part 5. (scenes 26-32) The climax of the play. The standards play an important part now – two sceptres and the two feathers are brought in. Finally the most important essential element of the crown, the gold headband, is brought in and the coronation takes place. A sacrifice is offered to the Great Ones of Upper and Lower Egypt who are ordered to approach and in their presence the Keeper of the Great Feather fixes the crown upon the newly proclaimed king. As a first act of bounty, the king distributes bread to the assembly.

Part 6. (scenes 33–46) The king's successor is transfigured in an extraordinary exchange – the new king symbolically embraces the old in a single ritual act. The king-who-will-rule dons a stomacher, a *Queni* around chest and back. Power accrues to the new king.

The divine power immanent in the old king is transferred to the new king. The son at the same time supports his father in his moment of transition. This ritualized embrace has another function. It signifies both the empowerment of the new king and the withdrawal of the old king who is considered to be undergoing his own transition. The embrace is retained while the mummy of the deceased king is prepared. Priestly officials called the Spirit-Seekers enact their own scene showing the king's ascent to heaven. Two priestesses bring food for the induction of the Spirit-Seekers into the Dual Shrines. The Spirit-Seekers convey the spirit of the king to the ancestral spirits. A great meal now took place. This served as a spell of prosperity for the reign which had been thus inaugurated.

This drama effected a real change of power. It was a true mystery. Through it, the king-who-would-rule had become king. Two transitions had been accomplished. Earthly power had been transferred to the new king in the embrace between father and son. The departed king, so strengthened in the embrace of his son, was in turn received in the heavenly embrace of his father in heaven. Pyramid Text 636 employs the same imagery.

> O, Osiris, this is Horus within thine arms.
> He will support thee.
> There is further transfiguration for him with thee.
> In thy name 'He of the Horizon from which
> Re goes forth.'
> Thou hast closed thy arms round him; round him
> He will not go away from thee.

CORONATION

The crown is more than an emblem, it replaces what is the human king's thinking, his destiny, personal character and in the case of the pharaoh, substitutes a Neter.

R. A. Schwaller de Lubicz, Sacred Science

A king is still empowered through the coronation ritual. Yet this crowning is essentially a secular affair despite the fact that it is conducted through the religious symbolism of our times. The coronation of the pharaoh marked not merely his accession to the throne but also his merging with the Neter Horus. Such an idea is incomprehensible to us. The pharoah was crowned as part of the Mystery Play of the Succession. We are able to reconstruct the main elements of the actual coronation rite from the Pyramid Texts, the Mystery Play of the Succession and Hatshepsut's temple at Deir el Bahri which gives us an insight into the significance of the sequence of events. It is no surprise to find the ever-present dual themes enacted at the coronation rite. The reconciliation of the dual lands represented by the dual crown was a continuous political theme. However the uraeus crown was more than a political symbol of might. It represented the role of the pharaoh as the holder of the fully raised kundalini powers. Every pharaoh was initiated into the mysteries of transformation through which the mortal nature was made divine. Frankfort describes the most essential element within the crown as the gold headband.

Coincidentally R. A. Schwaller de Lubicz expresses the same view. He maintains that it served as a symbolic dividing line between man and Neter, the personal and the divine. This arcane symbolism represents the culminating reality of Pharaonic theocracy, the full realization of the divine within the human. Schwaller de Lubicz further maintains that 'the king never carries out any act whatever, be it civil proceedings or a temple matter, without asserting that it is the Neter itself which is his inspiration'. Thus the individual personal will gave way to the divine will.

During the coronation rites, the pharaoh was also presented with the crook and flail. Finally, when 'the union of the two lands' was completed, the king undertook 'The Circuit of the

Walls', a circumambulation like beating the bounds used to demarcate territory. The Egyptians understood everything in terms of duality in balance: heaven and earth, north and south, the two lands, the two banks, the portions of Horus and Seth, the red crown and the white. These themes reappear time and time again in state ceremonial. Now that the succession was secured, the body of the deceased pharaoh could be finally buried. On the day before the coronation, the funeral of the past king took place. His resurrection was celebrated. The king was dead. Long live the king. The relationship between king and god was continuously upheld and nourished. It was sustained in the daily temple liturgy and renewed specifically at the *Hb Sd* festival.

THE HB SD FESTIVAL

Multifarious connections between gods and king, land and king, people and king were woven into that elaborate fabric which held society as well as the unaccountable forces of nature by strands which passed through the solitary figure on the throne of Horus.

Henri Frankfort, Kingship and the Gods

The term *Hb Sd* is represented by hieroglyphics which show two chapels placed side by side containing an empty throne placed on a dais. Here is an image of both duality and unity expressing the very essence of the ritual. The king's potency was renewed as ruler of both Lower and Upper Egypt. His sacred identification with the living Horus was mystically renewed. The festival took place on the same date as that used for ceremonies of coronation, the first day of the first month of the Season of Coming Forth, the first of Tybia.

The preparations for the festival were extensive. Often a complete new temple was founded. Courts were prepared to serve as the 'Court of the Festival' or 'Court of the Great Ones'. The Festival Hall, where the Great Throne stood, was constructed. Temporary shrines, 'Houses of the Sed Festival', were erected. A special construction, 'The Palace', was established where the ritual regalia was changed. The city holding the celebration was taken over, much like a modern day

Olympic host, by the activity of the festival. Barges arrived bearing statues of the gods. Officials arrived with their retinues from every part of the kingdom.

The festival opened with a torchlight procession formed by the king, the priesthood, statues of the gods and representatives from the secular community. The opening ceremonies were known as the Lighting of the Flame. Gifts were first offered to the minor gods as an acknowledgement for their participation. These initial proceedings were presided over by the goddess Sekhat-Hor, 'She Who Remembers Horus'. Two officials, bearing royal standards, the 'Hereditary Prince' and the 'Master of the King's Largess', directed the giving process. In the opening scenes of the reliefs of the temple of Osorkon II we see the pharaoh holding a clepsydra, a water clock. The renpet was also presented as a stripped and notched palm. It symbolizes time and the destiny of the king. The main deities were recognized through a more elaborate and personalized presentation. Their priesthoods appeared before the throne to pay homage. The king visited the individual shrines in the Court of the Great Ones.

The first two or three days were taken up with acts of homage at different levels. The priesthood offered homage to the king before the throne. The king descended from the throne and offered homage before the statue of the gods. During this period, the king undertook a specific cultic act known as 'Crossing the Field'. It is referred to in the texts as 'assuming the protection of the two lands'. The king crossed a piece of land symbolic of Egypt itself using an established pattern of movements, a choreographed step and a dancing fast, graceful walk. He completed the performance twice, once as the red king, once as the white king. All the while he was accompanied by a priest carrying the standard of Upwawet. He changed regalia at the 'Palace' and emerged wearing the short royal kilt and bull's tail and holding the symbolic house document which transfers ownership of the land. His kingship was not taken in the name of conquest but in the name of a rightful bequest. The concluding part of the festival was likewise dual in nature. He was empowered twice; his power was proclaimed twice. These five days of ceremony finally concluded with homage from the king to the minor deities not significantly active in the earlier proceedings. All was complete – the link between the ruler and the royal line was renewed.

Egyptologists used to regard the *hb sd* as a thirty-year jubilee of accession. This view is no longer thought to be accurate. We do not fully understand the significance of all the ritual acts and symbols but we can say that the king's relationship to the throne, the land, the people and the gods was renewed and re-established. In these arcane rituals the king was made. The vizier Rekhmire spoke rhetorically when he said, 'What is the king of Upper and Lower Egypt? He is a god by whose dealings one lives, the father and mother of all men, alone by himself, without equal.'

The Egyptian concept of kingship is truly beyond our grasp. Yet we can through meditation attempt to touch something of this historic reality. Let us imagine that we are to be present at the moment of crowning. Perhaps in this way we will gain an insight into the fusion of man and god which the Egyptians believed took place during the coronation. The meditation is written in the spirit of a mystery drama using some of the words spoken thousands of years ago.

THE MYSTERY OF SUCCESSION

Enter a state of meditation. You hold an important post and shall be honoured to be present at the coronation. You have been upon the barge with princes. You have marched to the mountains. The time is drawing close when the king-who-will-be, will be the king. All the preparations have been effected. It is time. You have studied long in the temple but there has not been a crowning in your lifetime. The Dual Shrines have been made ready. They stand back to back as one, each differentiated by its own standard. Upper and Lower Egypt stand ready. The king-who-was has passed into the kingdom of Osiris. The new king must rule the united lands. The crowns lie within the shrines. The priesthood awaits. The priest of Horus and Set, the two contestants, the two brothers, will grant legitimacy in reconciliation. Guardians stand at the doorways before the drawn veils hanging at the entrance to each shrine. The procession approaches. The king-who-will-rule leads. He is followed by dignitaries and the senior ranks among the priesthood. You take your place in the procession. With solemn and dignified pace the procession moves on.

You reach the place of the Dual Shrines. The pharaoh steps forward. The priest of Horus steps forward and conducts the king-who-will-be towards the shrine. The king enters the shrine of Wadjet. She is present in her shrine waiting for her son. The assembled hear the words as the Horus priest addresses the crown and the goddess immanent within it.

> The doors of the horizon are opened; their bolts are slipped.
> He comes to thee O Red Crown; he comes to thee O Fiery
> One.
> He comes to thee O Great One, he comes to thee O Magician.
> He has purified himself for thee
> Mayest thou be satisfied with him
> Mayest thou be satisfied with his purification
> Mayest thou be satisfied with the words he will say to thee:

The king-to-be addresses the crown on his own behalf:

> How beautiful is thy face, when thou art new and young.

The priest continues:

> A god has borne thee, the father of the gods;
> He (the king) comes to thee O Magician
> It is Horus who has fought to protect his eye O Magician
>   (Pyramid Text 194-5)

The pharaoh addresses the crown again:

> O Red Crown O Inu, O Great One,
> O Magician, O fiery Snake!
> Let there be terror of me like the terror of thee.
> Let there be fear of me like the fear of thee.
> Let there be awe of me like the awe of thee.
> Let there be love of me like the love of thee.

Let me rule a leader of the living.
Let me be powerful, a leader of spirits.
Let my blade be firm against my enemies.
O Inu, thou hast come forth from me;
and I have come forth from thee.

Thoth, the reconciler of Horus and Set, speaks while holding
the crown of Lower Egypt:

Take thou thine eye, whole to thy face.
Place it well in thy face.
Thine Eye shall not sadden with sadness
Take thou the fragrance of the gods (censing)
Through which cleanses, which has come out of thyself

The king is crowned. Thoth continues:

Cense thy face so that it be fragrant through
and through

The Priest of Horus speaks:

The Great One has borne thee
The exalted one has adorned thee;
For thou art Horus who has fought
For the protection of thine Eye

The Priest of Horus speaks while holding the crook:

Stand as king over it, over this land which has
come forth from Atum,
The spittle which has come forth from the beetle.
Be (king) over it; be high over it,
That thy father may see thee,
That Re may see thee.
He comes to thee, O father of his;
He comes to thee O Re!
Let him grasp the Heavens
And receive the Horizon
Let him dominate the Nine Bows
And equip (with offerings) the Ennead

Give the Crook into his hand
So that the head of Lower and Upper Egypt
shall be bowed

(Pyramid Texts 196-203)

The king is given the crook.

Now the king emerges. He will return to the second shrine there to homage the goddess Nekbet and receive her blessing. Soon the king-to-be will be king. The man will become the Neter. He will dispense bread and largesse and you may offer homage to the new incarnation of Horus.

Return to normal consciousness when you are ready.

7 · THE RITES FOR THE DEAD – NETER XERT

The mummies of ancient Egypt are living symbols of the transformative process of living and dying.

Normandie Ellis, Return to Egypt

Everyone is familiar with the Egyptian mummy. The word is derived from the Persian word 'moumia' meaning bitumen. A degree of desiccation naturally occurred in the hot dry sands. This simple observation was refined from the earliest primitive burials through time into the highskill of the embalmer's art. From ordinary and uninspiring beginnings, circular pits and preserved bodies, came the magnificent rock-cut tombs and the lavish cult of the dead.

We who bury our dead quickly and with little ceremony find it difficult to comprehend the motives of a people who bestowed such care on the dead. Contemporary funeral liturgy expresses our belief in the resurrection and the life to come. Individually we seem very uncertain about such matters. We hope for a resurrection, so we abandon the body quickly. The life of the body has finished. The Egyptians believed in the after-life but they could not abandon the body. It too was divine.

We cannot begin to comprehend the Egyptian cult of the

101

dead until we establish the Egyptian view of life. The funeral customs of a nation always reflect its philosophical stance. It is in the rites for the dead that we may assess the value placed on the living. The Egyptian cult of the dead shows us complexity, beauty and total commitment towards the life to come.

The Egyptians recognized a level of complexity in the human being that eludes our generally materialistic and rational outlook. We might grudgingly concede a polarity between body and soul, attributing the former to earthly existence and the latter to a heavenly existence. However even this simple duality exhausts the metaphysical vocabulary of a secularized society. By contrast the Egyptians held a complex metaphysical system. The divine and the human were reconciled in flesh.

At the most material level the Egyptians conceived of the *aufu*, the flesh body. This composed and integrated all other more subtle bodies. The divine was believed to be present in matter. The corporeal remains were referred to as the *khat*. This alone was without consciousness. The shadow or shade was referred to as *khabit*. The *sahu* was the body of gold. At the mental and emotional realms, the Egyptians described *sekhem* the will, *ren* the name and *ab* the heart, the seat of conscience. At spiritual levels we find the *ka*, the animating spirit, the *ba*, the immortal soul and *khu*, the divine intelligence. This hierarchy of being, from the physical to the spiritual, is not unlike that found in other metaphysical systems such as Qabalah.

The complexity takes us right into the burial chamber, the house of gold, where it was customary to place sarcophagus within sarcophagus, vehicle within vehicle. The mummified body of Tutankhamun, Strong-Bull-fitting-of-created-forms, Dynamic-of-Laws, Who-Calms-the-Two-Lands, Who-Propitiates-all-the-Gods, was laid in three coffins, a sarcophagus and four shrines.

The tomb of Tutankhamun gives us a glimpse of a splendour and glory beyond our imagining. This boy-king was an insignificant ruler, a pharaoh in the making, who was buried in a tomb originally prepared for another. His death was untimely, his funeral was unexpected. We can only imagine what glories tomb robbers have taken for ever. Yet in the tomb of a minor pharaoh we find exquisite beauty and craftsmanship beyond compare. This single complete tomb has shown us more than we could ever have hoped for. Here Tutankhamun rested within successive shrines, surrounded by the beautiful artefacts from everyday life and the symbols and images which promised resurrection.

Four shrines embraced the king's sarcophagus; each articulated the Egyptian belief in the life to come, through the sacred language of symbol and funerary text. Winged discs, symbols of liberation and rebirth, decorated the roof of the outermost shrine along with royal birds, the vulture and the falcon. The *tet* knot of Isis and the *djed* pillar of Osiris spoke of resurrection and well-being. Extracts from the Chapters of Coming Forth by Day were designed to empower the deceased. Underworld guardians were depicted to represent the forthcoming journey and its trials. The great funerary goddesses Isis and Nephthys stretched their wings in protective embrace.

These themes were continued upon the sarcophagus. Its roof showed a winged sun, a border of *tet* knots and *djed* pillars were inscribed around the base, the four protective goddesses Isis, Nephthys, Selkis and Neith stood in high relief, their wings outstretched to encompass the sides.

It is recorded that a gasp went up from the crowd of assembled dignitaries as the two sheets of covering linen were rolled back to reveal the outer coffin. Here was the face of Egypt in death. The coffin of cypress wood was modelled in relief with a thin layer of gesso overlaid with gold foil. Yet this was not the last resting place but only the first of three. The second coffin lay under floral offerings and proved to be even more magnificent than the first. It was inlaid with opaque glass to simulate carnelian, lapis lazuli and turquoise. The king held the crook and flail and wore the uraeus serpent crown along with the nemes head-dress, the traditional blue and gold striped headcloth. The third coffin was covered in a red linen shroud folded three times. The breast had been decorated with a collar of blue glass beads and various leaves and flowers. As the mummy itself was unwrapped 150 pieces of jewellery were revealed. These were fashioned and positioned according to the Chapters of Coming Forth by Day. Here were the ritual symbols, the scarab, the serpent, the falcon and the vulture in a glorious evocation of the transformation from the human to the divine.

The gold mask of the pharaoh is arguably the most beautiful artefact in the world. The many contents of this tomb, its magical items and personal effects, its royal regalia and ritual jewellery are not the trappings of morbidity but a celebration of life. There is no doubt that the Egyptians envisaged an after-life. In truth the physical life and the after-life were seen as a continuous thread unbroken at death. The tomb is a testament to the wholeness of life. It contains the familiar symbols of life in dazzling combination. In death the Egyptians show us beauty beyond compare. In death we see the total commitment to life. Nothing that had known life was dispensed ungraciously. Two tiny foetuses who never knew the fullness of life were placed in the tomb, each in a tiny mummy case. If the funeral rites of a society truly offer a reflected image what might future generations learn about the times in which we live?

In the Treasury was a second gilded shrine standing on a sled. This was the canopic shrine which contained the internal organs of the king. This elaborate and beautiful shrine with its protective goddesses has the inescapable air of a hallowed piece of work – even the individual organs were hallowed.

THE FOUR SONS OF HORUS

Children of Horus, Imset, Hapy, Duamutef, Qebhsenuf, as you spread your protection over your father Osiris, Foremost of the Westerners, so spread your protection over N.

Spell 137a

The liver, stomach, intestines and lungs were honoured by a separate and individual treatment. These organs were placed under the protection of the four sons of Horus. The four sons were themselves under the protection of a divinity. The human-headed Imset was assigned the liver under the protection of Isis. The lungs were assigned to baboon-headed Hapy, under the protection of Nephthys. Falcon-headed Qebhsenuf was assigned the intestines under the protection of Selkis. Finally the jackal-headed Duamutef was assigned the stomach under the protection of Neith. The four goddesses speak. Isis says, 'I conquer the foe, I make protection for Imset who is in me.' Nephthys says, 'I hide the thing, and I make protection for Hapy who is in me' Neith says 'I spend day and night of every day in making protection for Duamutef who is within me.' Selkis says, 'I employ each day in making protection for Qebhsenuf who is in me.' Spell 151 shows these four gods standing in the mummy chamber, one at each corner. Each of the four gods speaks. Imset says, 'I am your son, I have come that I may be your protection, and that I may make your house to flourish and endure, in accordance with the command of Ptah and in accordance with the command of Re.' Hapy says,' I have come that I may be your protection. I have knit together your head and your members. I have smitten your enemies beneath you, and I have given you your head for ever.' Qebhsenuf says, 'I am Quebhsenuf, I have come in order that I may be your protection. I join your bones together for you, I collect your members for you, and I bring your heart to you, I set it in its place in your body for you, and I have caused your house to flourish after you.' Duamutef says, 'I am your beloved son Horus, I have come that I may protect my father Osiris from him who would harm you, and lead him under your feet.'

RITES FOR THE DEAD

Hail to you, my ka of my lifetime; behold, I have come to you in glory, I am strong, besouled and mighty.

Spell 105

The cult of the dead which culminated in the construction of the places of ascension, the stairways to heaven, began humbly enough. The naturally desiccating effect of the hot, dry climate produced perfect conditions which cannot have gone unnoticed. In the First Dynasty there were clear attempts to improve upon the natural effect by wrapping the body with lengths of linen before burial. However it was obvious that decomposition still took place due to the processes of internal putrefaction. By the Fourth Dynasty it was common practice to remove the organs and keep them separate in canopic jars. From the earliest days it was customary to bury grave goods with the deceased. As wealth increased tombs became larger and more elaborate and security became a consideration. However these mastaba graves which stood above ground were an easy target for robbers. Wealthy tombs spawned ingenious tomb robbers. An early solution was to excavate underground chambers. Even during this early period burial was accompanied by ritual. The ceremony known as the Opening of the Mouth dates back to the Old Kingdom. All the elements that were to become the hallmarks of the Egyptian cult of the dead were in place, the mummy, the tomb and the ritual. The simple burial in drying sand became the glorious nest of sarcophagus and coffins one inside the other. The burial pit became the rock-cut tomb, the place of eternity. The ritual became the means of transformation from the human to the divine state. These three themes were elaborated, refined and woven into the very heart of the Egyptian psyche through centuries of trial and error.

Embalming clearly developed as a profession in its own right. At death the embalmers were called in by the family to carry the deceased to the *ibu*, the place of purification. The body was laid on matting outside in the sun covered with natron for four days. On the fourth day, it was taken into the *wabet*, the place of embalming. This was a temporary structure close to the necropolis. Here the corpse was washed in a ritualized operation symbolizing the rising of the sun from the Nile and the subsidence of the inundation waters. All the stages of the embalming process from first to last were accompanied by set rituals and formula. The embalmers were not mere technicians but a priesthood identified with the great mortuary god Anubis. At certain times the priests donned the jackal-headed mask and became Anubis, the great god of embalming. The chief embalmer, the Controller of the Mysteries, was assisted by the God's Spell Bearer who presented the appropriate spells throughout the process. The most senior priest was known as the Overseer of the Secrets of the Place. The minor priests who carried out the bandaging tasks were called *wtw*.

The Rhind Papyrus covers seventeen ceremonies, one for each of the seven openings in the head, the four viscera, two legs, two arms, chest and back. The tomb of Amenenope contained vignettes from the embalmers' workshop though representations of embalming are remarkably few. Two papyri from the Roman period give an insight into the rites which accompanied the embalming process. These documents are doubtless the Roman version of a very ancient tradition. The ceremonial aspect of the embalming was of the utmost importance. A purely technical procedure would have been finished in a far shorter time. The texts give precise instructions for each stage of the process. It is clear that embalming itself was part of the transformative process; each stage had a ritual significance. We can imagine the Anubis priests anointing the various parts of the body with oil, reciting the appropriate formula with a chanted resonance as they worked. We can also imagine the lengthy and sonorous formula which accompanied the placing of each protective amulet upon the body of the pharaoh Tutankhamun, *heqa-mat-sehetep-netjeru*, 'the one who brings cosmic order, who propitiates the gods'.

The embalming and mummification process began the ritual journey which was completed at the tomb itself. On the seventieth day the body was taken to its place of burial. (Is it mere coincidence that the stars Orion and Sirius were also invisible for 70 days before they re-emerged again reborn from the netherworld. Or is this yet again another example of the Egyptian's love of cosmic correspondence?) It was transported across the Nile by ferry. On the other side it was placed on a sledge drawn by oxen. The funeral procession set off towards the designated tomb. In the procession were the two mourners as Isis and Nephthys – professional mourners, relatives, a detachment of officials referred to as the Nine Friends, servants with tomb furniture and the funeral priests.

'A goodly burial arrives in peace, your seventy days having

been completed in your place of embalming, being placed upon the bier . . . and being dragged by young bulls, the road being opened with milk until you reach the door of your tomb. The children of your children, united with one accord, weep with loving hearts. Your mouth is opened by the lector-priest and your purification is performed by the Sem priest. Horus adjusts for you your mouth and opens for you your eyes and ears, your flesh and your bones being complete in all that appertains to you. Spells and glorifications are recited for you. There is made for you an Offering-which-the-King gives, your own heart being truly with you, your own heart of your earthly existence, you having arrived in your former state, as on the day on which you were born. There is brought to you the Son-whom-you-love, the courtiers making obeisance. You enter into land given by the king, into the sepulchre of the west.'

Outside the tomb the next ceremonial stage took place. The body was held upright at the entrance to the tomb. The ceremony of Opening of the Mouth was performed just outside the burial chamber. The mummy was raised to an upright position and purified with incense and water. The sem priest, the Son-whom-he-loves, performed the ceremonial restoration of the senses. The function of sem priest was originally carried out by the son in a cultic enactment of the relationship between Horus and Osiris as father and son. However in time the function was absorbed into the official priesthood. The priest touched the face twice with the adze and once with the pesesh-kef knife. The priest embraced the mummy to bring back its soul. The same ceremony was performed on the mummy of the pharaoh – all were united in death. Offerings of clothing, ointment and incense took place inside, followed by a small offering of food. The deceased was invited to join the assembly. A funeral feast followed and glorifications were recited by a lector priest. Finally, when the rites were completed, all footprints were swept away from the floor and the entrance was sealed. The deceased was not forgotten. If possible a small sum of money was made over to a mortuary priest, the servant of the ka, to provide daily offerings.

The body of Tutankhamun was wrapped in successive layers of linen strips. The mummy was laid in a succession of coffins. The three coffins were enclosed within a sarcophagus which was itself enclosed within four shrines. Every step of the process was accompanied by ritual; everything involved in the cult of the dead had symbolic value. The coffins and sarcophagus carried symbolic meaning too.

The first coffins were simply made of wood and were rectangular in shape. They were decorated to resemble the current architectural features with a slightly vaulted lid and recessed side panels. The earliest stone sarcophagi came from the Third Dynasty. The entire coffin but especially the lid was identified with Nut the sky goddess. The Pyramid Texts state 'you have been given to your mother Nut in her name of sarcophagus; she has embraced you in her name of coffin. And you have been brought to her in the name of tomb.' The floor represented the underworld. Inscriptions from the Coffin Texts which were derived from the royal Pyramid Texts were now included. By the Second Intermediate Period the anthropoid coffin which we naturally associate with the Egyptian mummy was well established. Decorative conventions came into use which portrayed the ever-occurring themes of renewal and rebirth through symbolic images. The protective wings of various goddesses became an important feature of the *rishi*, 'feathered' style. The decorative schema which included the depiction of a broad jewelled collar and a winged scarab representing the sun god were painted over the upper chest.

There were four registers of further decoration. The first register showed Horus bringing the deceased into the presence of the four protective deities, often Isis, Osiris, Nephthys and Thoth. The next register showed Isis and Nephthys with outstretched wings and above them the winged disc of the sun. In the third register Isis and Nephthys in human form stand on either side of the djed pillar. In the fourth register Horus and Thoth pour a stream of lustrations in the form of *ankhs* and *was* sceptres over the deceased. Under this last register was a large vulture and a horizontal band of text containing prayers and food offerings. 'Your mother Nut has spread herself over you, she has caused you to become a god, your enemies do not exist.' The burial chamber too symbolized the entire cosmos. The sarcophagus planted upon the floor was once again the primeval mound waiting to spring to life.

The Egyptians believed unequivocally in a life beyond the grave. Every symbol from the *djed* pillar to the winged Isis, from the *ankh* to the lotus affirmed the continuity of life unbroken by death. The coffin held the deceased like a cocoon holding its secret of transformed existence. The sarcophagus, like the hard protective covering over the seed, permitted the germination of new life within. The seed was planted upon the primeval mound, the archetypal mound of creation. Everything affirmed the new life. The rituals which began in the place of embalmment and were completed in the burial chamber enacted the process of transformation. The physical body could serve no longer. The non-physical body which was always considered to be present was awakened, consciousness was transferred from one to the other. The means for achieving this transfer of consciousness were laid down in a collection of formulae known collectively as *reu nu pert em hru*, Chapters of Coming Forth by Day.

ON COMING FORTH BY DAY

I have come, even I the vindicated Osiris N, on business of the Lord of All.

Spell 1b

Our unwillingness to allow the Egyptians to speak for themselves manifests again. We insist on referring to the chapters Coming Forth by Day as the Book of the Dead. The Egyptians would not have recognized their work by our title. The difference in meaning between the two titles is considerable. The texts, usually referred to as spells, were intended to guide the soul through the underworld. The corpus of spells, nearly two hundred altogether, formed a repertoire from which the individual commissioned a personal selection. These were then transcribed. However if money or time did not permit a choice, a ready-made selection could be purchased. Copies were placed in the coffin or between the layers of linen.

The earliest papyri date from the mid-fifteenth century BC but they include the beliefs from a thousand years earlier. The totality of the slowly changing Egyptian belief system is represented somewhere in the chapters of Coming Forth by Day.

Some texts originated in the Pyramid Texts, others refer to the Opening of the Mouth. Certain texts refer to the supremacy of the sun god Re, other texts refer to Osiris. This collection covered thousands of years of religious tradition; it permitted the individual a totally free and personal choice. The collection was modernized when the priesthood of Heliopolis compiled two works, The Book of What is in the Underworld, *shat am tuat*, and the Book of Gates, *shat en sbau*. These presented two quite different theologies. The Book of What is in the Underworld gave supremecy to Amen Ra. In the Book of Gates, Osiris is given the greater importance. The one theology depicts the sun god's journey through the various regions and its infernal monsters led by Apep. This theology recounts the familiar theme of battle between light and darkness. The Osirion theology is far more personal and was probably far more popular. Here we find perhaps the most famous Egyptian scene of all, the Judgement Hall.

THE HALL OF MAAT

Hail to you great lord of justice. I have come to you my lord that you may bring me so that I may see your beauty for I know you and I know your name and know the names of the forty-two gods of those who are with you in the Hall of Justice.

Spell 125

The Egyptian anticipated the Judgement Hall, the place of accounting where the life of the heart was weighed against the feather of truth. The Judgement Hall is described in the Papyrus of Ani. The deceased Ani enters the hall with his wife. Ani appeals to his heart not to betray him. For his heart will be weighed and the result will be recorded by Thoth.

111

Ani opens with the traditional Declaration of Innocence, the Negative Confession.

I have done no falsehood
I have not robbed
I have not stolen
I have not killed men
I have done no crookedness
I have not stolen the god's-offering
I have not told lies
I have not taken food
I have not been sullen
I have not transgressed
I have not killed a sacred bull
I have not committed perjury
I have not stolen bread
I have not eavesdropped
I have not babbled
I have not disputed except as concerned my own property
I have not committed homosexuality
I have not misbehaved
I have not made terror
I have not transgressed
I have not been hot tempered
I have not been deaf to the words of truth
I have not made disturbance
I have not hoodwinked
I have neither misconducted myself nor copulated with a
    boy
I have not been neglectful
I have not been quarrelsome
I have not been unduly active
I have not been impatient
I have not washed out the picture of a god
I have not been voluble in speech
I have done no wrong
I have seen no evil
I have not made conjuration against the king
I have not waded in water
I have not been loud voiced
I have not reviled god
I have not made distinctions for myself

I am not wealthy except with my own property
I have not blasphemed God in the city.

> Spell 125, The Chapters of Coming Forth by Day

Thus the deceased declared his innocence and prepared to meet Osiris. Let us do the same in meditation.

The Weighing of the Heart

Enter your own meditative state. Your life on earth is over. You find yourself standing in the white linen of the deceased. You find yourself standing outside a pair of closed double doors. Each door has the sign of the ankh engraved upon it. The doors are pushed open from within; you stand back. The jackal-headed god Anubis steps through and takes you by the hand. 'I am Governor of the Hall of the God', he says. You enter together and find yourself standing in a large hall. The cornice is formed of uraeii picked out in bright colours and the symbol of Maat, the white feather. On either side of the hall, seated in long rows, sit the Forty-Two Assessors, twenty-one on each side. In the centre of the hall stands a set of scales; at the top of the central support is carved the figure of Maat wearing the white feather. You know that these are her scales. You see Thoth holding the scribal palette – he will record the verdict. You see Ammit the Devourer waiting. The hall is absolutely still. There is no sound except that made by your footsteps upon the floor. Anubis seems to make no sound at all as he crosses the hall.

You remember all the teachings that you received in life, and you remember what you will say. You begin and your voice hangs in the air. All heads incline to you. All eyes are upon you. 'Hail to you great god lord of justice, I have come to you my lord that you may bring me so that I may see your beauty, for I know you and I know your names and I know the names of the forty-two gods of those who are in this Hall of Justice.' You begin your declaration of innocence. As you speak, you address each god in turn and after each affirmation the god nods without speaking. With every statement, images come to mind of people and places, circumstances and situations. Your words falter with the heaviness of remembrance. You finish the declaration of innocence.

A deep silence falls on the hall. Anubis moves forward. He checks the balance, making sure that the tongue is equally balanced favouring neither outcome. He checks that the beam is exactly horizontal. All is ready. Anubis returns to his place beside you and as if from nowhere produces a vase which he holds carefully between his two hands. As he moves slowly towards the balance, the memories of the spiritual heart within you begin to stir. You remember the life of the heart, its opening to love and to life and its tremors of fear. You remember the pain of the heart, too, its woundedness and pain. You wonder if your heart will prove to be as cold and hard as stone? You hope not, for you believe that in honesty you nourished the life of the heart as best you could.

Anubis has reached the balance. He places the small vase on the ground beside one pan of the scales. He takes the white feather from the carved figure of Maat with the other. He holds it aloft for all to see. You gaze upon the feather and remember Maat, she who is straight. The feather looks so light. Anubis drops the feather. It falls slowly through the air and disappears into the depth of the golden pan. The pointer on the scales does not move. The pan does not move. Anubis picks up the vase which contains the heart's knowing. He raises it aloft then places it carefully in the second pan with all the tenderness of a mother laying a child in a cradle. For a moment the two pans seem to quiver as if adjusting to one another. Thoth steps forward in anticipation. The pans have settled. The tongue of the balance is perfectly centred. All is balanced with the life that has just finished. Thoth records the verdict.

Thoth announces the verdict to the assembly. 'The Osiris scribe is justified, is righteous. He has committed no crime nor has he acted against us. Ammit shall not be permitted to prevail over him. Let there be given to him bread offerings which go before Osiris and a permanent grant of land in the fields of offerings.'

Spell 30b, The Chapters of Coming Forth by Day

Anubis steps forward again. He will be your guide to the regions of this new world. He gently takes your arm and you begin to walk together towards the far end of the hall. As you draw closer, you see that the guardians of the hall are drawing back the bolts. The doors open, a blaze of light fills the hall, you walk on with Anubis at your side and pass out of the hall of judgement into the light beyond. You return to normal consciousness with the full memory of your experience.

8 · THE MYSTERIES OF THE GODS AND GODDESSES – NETER AND NETERIT

No land can lay claim to such a chronicle of mystical and occult thought as Egypt, the mother of magic.
Lewis Spence, The Mysteries of Egypt

The Egyptians had no word for worship in the sense that we understand it today. Egyptian practice went far deeper than prayer and praise. The word *iau* specifically implies the establishment of a relationship between object and subject, Neter and participant. It is an interaction of identification and assimilation between the participant and the Neter. This process is at the heart of the Mysteries.

Our difficulty yet again is one of finding equivalence. It is confusing enough when we have to redefine contemporary terms to incorporate a wider or quite different Egyptian meaning. Yet to penetrate the heart of the Mysteries we have to absorb concepts that have no contemporary equivalent at all. To comprehend the Mysteries of Egypt we must make a quantum leap.

Egyptian vocabulary may provide some clues as to intent and purpose. The word *iau* indicates the nature of a dynamic relationship between the Neter and the individual. The word *sheta* means mystery. In daily usage it means 'hidden', 'concealed', or 'unprecedented'. In its religious context it means a truly religious secret. The word *djeser* is usually translated as 'magnificent' and 'exalted'. However it too has an additional meaning. It means 'secluded', 'inaccessible' or 'hidden'. Finally the verb *bes* means 'to usher in' or 'to enter', in other words 'to initiate'. This word is used for the investiture of the pharaoh, the installation of a priest and an initiation into the secrets of a cult. It can also be used to refer to the mystery itself.

Here are the four words which can provide us with the clues that may take us to the heart of the mystery. What were these 'religious secrets', these 'secluded, hidden, inaccessible, magnificent, exalted experiences'? What were the Egyptian Mysteries?

The word mystery is derived from the Greek *myein* meaning 'to close', referring to the lips or eyes. This symbol has been much misunderstood. The essence of the Mysteries was never a secret but an experience, and a transcendent experience cannot be put into words. A description of such an experience provides no more than a narration, a commentary of words. It is impossible to convey the depth of feeling and intensity of emotion experienced as awe, wonder, holy terror, divine rapture and ecstatic bliss. Without experience it is impossible for an individual to imagine such states of intensity. With experience it is impossible for the individual to convey the intensity of the event. There is no common meeting point. The result is a silence imposed not by a desire to exclude, but generated from the impossibility of bridging the gap in experience through words alone.

Our contemporary problem does not come from a lack of information. We have the recorded accounts of several eye witnesses; travellers, scholars, writers and even those who were accepted into the Mysteries themselves. But we have lost the context through which we may fully understand the significance of these accounts. If we try to set these accounts against a modern religious landscape, we shall be none the wiser. Herodotus recorded the public festivals which he witnessed.

> The Egyptians hold public festivals not only once in a year, but several times: that which is best and most rigidly observed, is in the city of Bubastis, in honour of Diana: The second, in the city of Busiris, is in honour of Isis and is situated in the middle of the Egyptian delta. Isis in the Grecian language is called Demeter. The third festival is held at Sais, in honour of Minerva; the fourth, at Heliopolis in honour of Latona, the fifth, at the city of Papremis, in honour of Mars . . . In the city of Sais they all on a certain night kindle a great number of lamps in the open air, around their houses; the lamps are flat vessels filled with salt and oil, and the wick floats on the surface, and this burns all night, and the festival is thence named the 'lighting of lamps . . . At Sais also, in the sacred precinct of Minerva, behind the chapel and adjoining the whole of the wall, is a tomb of one whose name I consider it impious to divulge on such an occasion. And in the enclosure stand large stone obelisks, and there is a lake nearby, ornamented with a stone margin, formed in a circle, and in size, as appeared to me much the same as that at Delos which is called the Circular. In this lake they perform by night the representation of that person's adventures which they call mysteries. On these matters, however, though accurately acquainted with the particulars of them, I must observe a discreet silence.

In this short report Herodotus has laid out the bare bones of the Egyptian Mysteries for us. It is clear that he was present at a dramatic representation of the story of the Osiris. The decorum displayed by so voracious a reporter is indicative that he was willing to conform to the Egyptian custom. It has been widely suggested that he was himself ushered into these mysteries.

We may wonder what could be secret about a play, a simple piece of drama. Sacred drama is not so far from the European inheritance. Mediaeval mystery plays brought great Biblical themes to the populace. The Egyptians too were well aware of the educative function of drama. However they were also aware of another more subtle function, namely its power to initiate. The two functions have become separate as part of the great divide between the secular and the sacred. Sacred drama has evolved into church ritual, by comparison a pale imitation of the Egyptian prototype. Profane drama has evolved into varied and sometimes nefarious forms. However even profane drama has the power to move the emotions and create a change of perspective which is the key to all acts of initiation.

The Egyptians offered both levels of dramatic enactment. The public witnessed and indeed participated in drama which re-enacted their own mythology. These open dramas were the exoteric rites. The priesthood performed more intense, more complex versions of the same stories for themselves. These were the esoteric rites. The function of these rites was to enable the candidate to encounter the presence of the Neter at increasingly more intense levels. In a civilization dominated by themes of duality, it is no surprise to find inner and outer rite, public and private ceremony.

IMPERSONATING THE GODS

It is difficult to explain to anyone who has no experience of this peculiar magical rite, which is known as the assumption of a god-form, what effect this operation has on the operator and on those working with him.

C. R. F. Seymour, The Forgotten Mage

The esoteric and exoteric rites may have told the same story at a different level. Yet a gulf lay between these two presentations. The populist rites were attended and orchestrated by the priesthood. Such spectacles like great music, theatre or religious assembly doubtless had an emotional and uplifting effect. This was enough. The priestly rite, enacted by a small class of specialized personnel who acted as impersonators of the gods, was a revelation of a cosmic principle. Such ceremony was sharply focused, its effect was calculated and specific. These rites expressed the Egyptian understanding of worship, *iau*, the dynamic relationship between initiate and Neter. This relationship was built up gradually through three phases; recognition, identification and assimilation. The first stage, recognition, was achieved through entry into the symbolism of a particular cult. The second stage, identification, was established through participation in the dramatic enactments. The impersonator of the god took on the qualities of the god. The Horus priest embodied Horus, the priest of Osiris was Osiris, the priestess of Hathor was Hathor herself. Identifying with the cult divinity is not a matter of acting but of absorbing the qualities attributed to the divinity. It cannot be achieved intellectually. Analytical thinking always produces a gulf between the individual and the thought. Identification is achieved only through total absorption, it is a union generated by the heart.

Taking on the identity of the Neter is not a totally lost art. It is clear that Seymour was speaking from experience when he wrote 'the whole of these magical rituals and rites derived their effectiveness from the ability of the officiating priest or priestess to identify himself with the god (goddess) being personified'. He saw this ancient practice made real.

The third and final stage, assimilation, occurred through total symbiosis between the human participant and the Neter. This was a state of mystical union. Total identification carried the participant towards what Seymour calls the 'direct contact with the numen' and 'the central mystery of initiation'. It was the mystical experience, the heart of the mysteries. Such things cannot be discussed but not from coyness or reticence – there are no useful words. We have simply come a full circle. The starting point was the initiatory recognition, the culmination was the mystical absorption into the Neter. Thus *iau* was achieved.

When we are describing the Mysteries it is important to remember that we are only describing the vehicle of revelation, not the mystery itself. We cannot know how individuals were changed through their participation in the sacred dramas. We may however conclude that sacred dramas were the vehicle for personal change.

The most famous Mysteries were those of Isis and Osiris. Isis herself says, 'I revealed Mysteries unto men'. These Mysteries were divided into the Lesser and Greater. The Lesser Mysteries were associated with the wanderings of Isis and the Greater Mysteries were associated with the resurrection of Osiris.

The Lesser Mysteries

In the lesser mysteries, the neophyte was taught by means of meditation and ritual the art of centering on the 'Isis within'. He learned the techniques of going into the silence, and of waiting until the goddess herself appeared to him.

Seymour, The Forgotten Mage

The various cult rituals represented the sorrows and sufferings of Isis as she searched for the lost Osiris. This enactment served to awaken the emotions and open the heart. The symbolic quest for the beloved goes far beyond the personalized quest of a wife for her husband. It represents the search for meaning, the search for self and the search for the greater whole. The quest is the archetypal and universal motif for the first stage in spiritual seeking. This journey is always the starting point. The Lesser Mysteries awakened the subconscious mind. In these mysteries the student was awoken to Isis as the mother of Wisdom and Compassion.

The Greater Mysteries

Through the mysteries people glimpsed the true nature of the cosmos and of themselves.

Arthur Versluis, The Egyptian Mysteries

The Mysteries of Osiris depicted the finding and resurrection of Osiris. If the first stage represented seeking, the second stage represented finding. This theme was literally enacted in the Hilaria, The Day of Joy. During this four-day festival actors impersonated the divinities Isis, Nephthys and Anubis and searched for the body of Osiris. On the final day the cry went up, 'we have found, we rejoice together'. Osiris was found, the search was complete. In this Romanized and public version of a mystery teaching, the theme of the quest was played out. Outside Egypt, removed from the fountainhead of wisdom, impersonating the divinities and mediating the divine god-forms had sunk to a pale imitation of the original. Nevertheless the symbolized finding of Osiris represents the next stage of the quest. Genuine seeking leads to finding and precipitates the first birth into the spiritual life. Separation is replaced by unification. This process of searching and unification gives birth to a new level of consciousness, the Horian revelation. Horus is conceived between the worlds where all spiritual gestations begin. We know little of the Isian Mysteries in Egypt itself. We know rather more about the Mysteries of Osiris.

THE MYSTERIES OF OSIRIS

The actual significance and purpose of the Mysteries of Egypt was a preparation for the higher life, for a more exalted spiritual existence after death.

Lewis Spence, The Mysteries of Egypt

We find two parallel sets of rites, the public and the priestly, the exoteric and the esoteric, the arcane and the mundane. Both took the form of enacted dramas. Herodotus clearly attended mystery plays which concerned the life, death and resurrection of Osiris. This theme was presented in wholly human terms for the populace at large. They were invited to empathize with the life of this good god, to mourn his murder, to search for his body as Isis herself had done and finally to rejoice at his resurrection. The cycle of his life was celebrated throughout the year in exactly the same way that the Christian calendar revolves around the birth, death and resurrection of Christ.

His festivals were universally celebrated through every Nome in the land. The month of Khoiakh was dedicated to him. All the symbolic enactments of the month displayed the theme of rebirth. A hollow effigy of Osiris was filled with barley and sand. It was watered and placed in the sun. The Osiris from the previous year was raised from its sepulchre and placed on sycamore twigs. The *Djed* column was raised representing the resurrection of Osiris. This level of enactment was simple and populist.

At Abydos the public rites were full-blooded. We have a wonderful account of the proceedings. Ikhernofret, an officer who took the key role of Horus, described the drama on a memorial stone. We need to imagine the intense activity as people arrived from all over the country and prepared to take sides.

Eight acts took place over seven days. In the first act the jackal-headed god Upwawet prepared the way for the appearance of Osiris. 'I celebrated the procession of Upwawet', says Ikhernofret. Osiris appeared in the second act in a sacred barque. However the voyage was duly interrupted by the enemies of the god, dressed as Set and his cohorts. Battle took place. 'I repulsed those who were hostile to the Neshmet barque, and I overthrew the enemies of Osiris,' says Ikhernofret. Both Ikhernofret and Herodotus, who witnessed the same events some fifteen hundred years later, are silent about the details of the death of Osiris which took place in the third act. In the fourth act, Thoth searched for the body. In the fifth act, the body was prepared for burial. As Horus, Ikhernofret procured the sacred barque, a ship-shaped sledge built from sycamore and acacia decorated with gold, silver and lapis lazuli. Inside he installed the statue of the god. The burial procession made its way across the desert. 'I equipped the barque, *Shining in Truth*, of the Lord of Abydos, with a chapel; I put on his beautiful regalia when he went forth to the district of Peker.' The funeral way was again obstructed by the followers of Set. Finally, in the sixth act, Osiris was placed in his tomb accompanied by the populace who marched out into the desert to watch the god being laid to rest. In the seventh act a final battle took place on a lake between the followers of Horus and the followers of Set. 'I championed Wennofer on That Day of the Great Battle, I overthrew all the enemies upon the shore of Nedyt,' says Ikhernofret. The outcome was of course inevitable. Yet battle was joined with great gusto on both sides and men were injured. At last Osiris was restored to life amidst a triumphal procession and his resurrection was seen to be complete.

Thus were the mysteries of Osiris celebrated at Abydos. This extraordinary mix of priesthood and populace created a seven-day human drama which moved from one landscape to another, using water, desert and mountains like a backdrop. Contending sides fought like a rugby scrum. The populace knew the story of Osiris, they had fought his enemies in his defence. Through this wild and intensely human involvement the populace came to know the stories of their gods. Through its inner form the priesthood came to know the gods themselves.

The priestly proceedings were of an altogether different nature. The drama of the death of Osiris was celebrated on the first of the month of Paschons. His resurrection was enacted on the 22nd of Thoth. In the intervals, the priesthood performed the interior ceremonies in private. By contrast to the great and often rowdy public festivities, these rites took place at tiny shrines. At Philae, the drama of the death and resurrection of Osiris was celebrated not in a week but in the space of one day. The story was described through twenty-four scenes, one for each hour of both day and night. Accordingly the rite began on the first hour of the night at 6 o'clock and concluded at the same time the next day. Each hour contained its own drama. The drama moved from the death and attendant lamentations to the resurrection.

The rite is depicted at the temple. Osiris is shown first in his mummy form, enveloped in a funeral shroud upon a bier. The mummy is surrounded by ritual regalia, crowns, sceptres, vases containing myrrh and other fumigations. Shou, Geb, Horus, Anubis, Isis and Nephthys were each represented by a member of the priesthood. The drama unfolded as texts were recited in formal and solemn fashion. The goddesses Isis and Nephthys lamented through the mediation of two priestesses. After the long lamentations, the drama proceeded to its next phase. At the sixth hour a vase containing water from the Nile was brought in. Osiris himself was often likened to Nile water. The process of resurrection began when the body of Osiris was sprinkled with this sacramental water. Osiris passed to heaven accompanied by his ka. The gods themselves reassembled the dismembered Osiris. First the skeleton was assembled, followed by the flesh. The soul was recalled through magnetic passes. The completed body was restored through holy water, oils and unguents. The drama proceeded. On the sixth hour of the day, the *Djed* pillar was raised. At midday when the sun was at its height Osiris was fully restored. The pharaoh himself brought offerings. At the twelfth hour the rite was finished, lamps were lit, the doors were opened. The god was resurrected.

Other divinities had their celebrations too. The voyage of Hathor to Edfu was another event on a grand scale. In this way the ordinary Egyptian people participated in the divine life of the nation.

Let us now touch upon the spirit of the Mysteries. In meditation let us encounter the experience of personal trial.

THE HALL OF OSIRIS

Enter your own meditation. You are at Abydos in the temple of Osiris. You have spent time in preparation for this day. You have spent time in meditation, study and contemplation. Today you shall be received into the Osirion – the death place, and the birth place.

You stand just outside the door in the west wall of the Chapel of Osiris. The door is closed, you wait to be summoned into the Osirion. You remember everything you have been taught. The door is opened and you enter the first hall of Osiris.

You have heard of this place but you have never been here before. Torches burn, casting strange flickering shadows on the wall. This is the underworld. The air here is cool, you can smell water upon stone and stone upon water. Ahead, you see the dark thread of water encircling the island. You stand perfectly still, taking in your surroundings. Here on this bank you retain a link with the living.

You are close to the realm of the netherworld. Soon you shall cross the divide. You recall your earthly life and all that it has been to you up to this moment in time. Your mind is steady, your heart is pure. You step across the water with a firm step and stand in the netherworld. You have gone beyond life. You stand upon the island which is both your death and your birth. You see the canopic vases laid out. Here upon the island, the open sarcophagus waits for you. You know what you must do. You know that someone here in the darkness is watching you.

Step forward and lie down in its cold embrace. All is black.
All is cold.

An unseen hand extinguishes the torches. You remember
that Osiris too was entombed within a casket. You know that
upon the inside of the sarcophagus are carved texts from the
Chapters of Coming Forth by Day. You know the Chapters by
heart. A rising fear creeps over you but you dispel it and con-
centrate the mind. You sink more deeply into concentration.
The body grows colder. Time seems suspended. There are no
markers of time or directions. You fold your arms over your
chest and feel your beating heart. You begin to recite the words
in your mind. Your mind opens, the body seems far away. You
address Osiris in whose name you have come:

> Hail to you, Starry One in Heliopolis; Sun-folk in Kheraha;
> Wenti more powerful than the god; Mysterious One in
> Heliopolis.
> Hail to you, Heliopolitan in Iun-des; Great One; Horakhty
> the Far-Strider when he crosses the sky: he is Horakhty.
> Hail to you, Ram of Eternity, Ram who is Mendes, Wennefer
> son of Nut: he is Lord in the Silent Land.
> Hail to you in your rule of Busiris, the Weret-crown is firm
> on your head:
> You are the Sole One who makes his own protection,
> and you rest in Busiris.
> Hail to you, Lord of the naret-tree; Sokar is placed on his
> sledge, the rebel who did evil is driven off, and the Sacred
> Eye is at rest in its place.
> Hail to you, strong in power, the great and mighty one who
> presides over Naref, Lord of Eternity, maker of everlastingness:
> you are Lord of Heracleopolis.
> Hail to you, who are pleased with justice: you are Lord of
> Abydos, and your flesh has enriched the Sacred Land; you
> are he who detests falsehood.
> Hail to you, occupant of the Sacred Bark, who brings the
> Nile from its cavern, over whose corpse the sun has shone;
> you are he who is in Nekhen.
> Hail to you who made the gods, the vindicated King of
> Upper and Lower Egypt, Osiris,
> who founded the Two Lands with his potent deeds: you are
> Lord of the Two Banks.

May you give me a path that I may pass in peace, for I am
straightforward and true; I have not wittingly told lies, I
have not committed a second fault.

> Spell 15, Chapters of Coming Forth by Day

It seems to you in the dark and the cold and silence that a
voice within speaks.

Hail unto you seeker of Osiris,
Hail unto you child of earth,
Hail unto you traveller in eternity,
You have found me for I am here.
This is my kingdom where all is renewed in the darkness.
You shall be renewed too for you have not travelled in vain.
You shall see me as I see you.

Another voice sounds in your head.

'To which god shall I announce you?'
'To him who is now present. Tell it to the Dragoman of the
Two Lands.'
'Who is the Dragoman of the Two Lands?'
'He is Thoth.'
'Come!' says Thoth. 'What have you come for?'
'I have come here to report'.
'What is your condition?'
'I am pure from evil. I have excluded myself from the
quarrels of those among you who are now living. I am not
among them.'
'To whom shall I announce you?'
'You shall announce me to Him whose roof is fire, whose
walls are living ureai, the floor of whose house is the water.'
'Who is he?'
'He is Osiris.'
'Proceed; behold, you are announced. Your bread is the
Sacred Eye, your beer is the Sacred Eye; what goes forth at
the voice for you upon earth is the Sacred Eye.'

> Spell 125, Chapters of Coming Forth by Day

You see a pair of huge doors each inscribed with an ankh.
They open before you. At the far end sits Osiris with crook

and flail. You approach the doors but they close before you reach them. Yet you have seen Osiris this day. A voice says, 'Not now, beloved, return.'

Your body jolts. You do not think you can move. You have lost all sense of time. Torchlight flickers somewhere. In the darkness faces peer over. Strong arms reach in and lift you. A voice says, 'Our beloved has travelled far.' Your body is rigid with cold but your mind is vitalized. When you are fully returned, you will give the report of your experiences here in the Hall of Osiris.

In Conclusion

You have come in search of Wisdom. You alone will know whether you feel that you have touched upon something real and significant. The Wisdom of Egypt is not dead. It has invisibly shaped the history of the world. We stand at a point in time when technology threatens to outpace wisdom. We are a world much in need of wisdom. Perhaps the sages of the past still have something to teach us. The Wisdom of Egypt is not dead but eternal. The following meditation may put you in touch with the living current which still lives.

I wish you well on your journey into Wisdom. You can only be enriched by your search.

THE BARQUE OF THE GODS

Descend into meditation. It is deep night. There are stars above you. The air is warm. You realize that you are far above the ground. You stand at the top of what we know as the Great Pyramid, The Place of Ascension. You remember that once these blocks were clad in brilliant white. That brilliance is now gone.

You stand high in this place contemplating all that you have learned. There are many questions in your mind. You enter more deeply into your own thoughts. You are surrounded by the night sky. You remember the hour-men of old. You see the great constellation of Orion and you long to understand. You ask from deep within yourself that you might be blessed to receive a revelation.

You watch the night sky with your inner eye. It seems that you see a movement among the stars. As you watch, from the starry background there emerges a boat. It is the Boat of Stars, the Barque of the Gods, the Boat of Millions of Years. You pay close attention. You affirm your aspiration. The barque seems to become clearer.

It is moving across the night sky in a slow and graceful arc. The Neters stand within the boat. You call out from your heart and ask for a blessing. Your voice is heard, for the boat stops and the gods look down upon you.

In the prow you see ibis-headed Thoth. 'Seek wisdom,' he says. Beside him is Maat with her white feather. 'Uphold truth,' she says. Next you see Isis wearing the symbol of the throne. 'Enter my service,' she says. Beside her is Osiris. 'Believe in resurrection,' he says. Standing behind them is the falcon-headed Horus. 'Seek the second birth.' Next you see Hathor, the golden one. 'Create beauty,' she says. With her is Set. 'Pierce duality,' he says. Last you see Anubis. 'Open the ways and go forth'.

Then all the gods turn to face you. In a single gesture the Great Company raise their hands in salutation and it seems to you that starlight pours through them and bathes your being in a brilliant irridescence. You look to yourself but momentarily and when you return to the night sky the barque is gone. All is silent. You give thanks and reflect deeply and return to normal consciousness when you feel ready.

GLOSSARY

GLOSSARY OF EGYPTIAN TERMS

Ab, the heart, the seat of conscience.
Ankh, the key of life.
Aufu, the flesh body.
Ba, the immortal soul.
Bes, to usher in, or to enter, to initiate.
Djed, pillar, symbol of resurrection.
Djeser, magnificent, exalted, secluded, inaccessible or hidden.
Duat, also called **Tuat**, the underworld.
Hat nub, the house of gold.
Hbn shn nfr, the festival of the beautiful embrace
Hb Sd, a state festival of kingly renewal.
Heq, the crook.
Heqa-Iuna-Shema, the living image of Amun – title of Tutan-khamun.
Heqa-mat-sehetep-netjeru, the one who brings cosmic order, who propitiates the gods – title of Tutankhamun.
Hm, body, physical appearance, usually translated as majesty.
Hm ka, 'the servant of the ka', the funerary priests.
Hm ntr, the servants of the god.
Iau, the relationship between object and subject, Neter and worshipper.
Ibu, the place of purification
Imy-wnwt, the 'hour watcher' priest.

Ka, the animating spirit.

Khabit, the shadow or shade.

Khat, the corporeal remains.

Kheri-heb, 'the possessor of the book', the 'lector priests'.

Khu, the divine intelligence.

Medu Neter, 'the signs of the gods', hieroglyphics.

Menat, beaded collar worn by the priestesses of Hathor.

Medjty, the priest of the private clothing.

Mer, the Place of Ascension, Egyptian term for pyramid.

Merkhert, 'the instrument of knowing' used for stellar observation.

Mwt, mother.

Nb. t smj. t, Mistress of the western desert, a title of Hathor.

Nb. t nht, Mistress of the sycamore, a title of Hathor.

Nekhak a, the flail

Neter, god, universal power.

Nebkheprure, the lordly manifestation of Re

Per aa, the pharaoh, the great house.

Per ankh, the House of Life.

Per Ht-hr, Hathor's temple at Denderah, The House of Hathor.

Pesesh-kef, knife, ritual instrument used in the Opening of the Mouth.

Queni, the ritual stomacher worn in the mystery of succession.

Ren, the name.

Renpet, the notched palm branch symbolic of a measure of time.

Reu nu pert em hru, the Chapters of Coming Forth by Day.

Rishi, a 'feathered' style of decoration used on the mummy case

Sahu, the body of gold.

Sekhem, the will, also a baton of authority.

Sem, the priest who performed the ceremony of Opening the Mouth.

Shat am tuat, the Book of What is in the Underworld.

Shat e sbau, the Book of Gates.

Sheta, mystery.

Sistrum, the sacred rattle

Sma, the symbol for union.

Tet, the knot of Isis

Wab, 'the purified ones', the basic rank of the priesthood.

Wabet, the place of embalming.

Was, sceptre, ritual sceptre denoting duality.

Wp mpt, the opener of the year.

Wtw, the minor embalming priests.

GLOSSARY OF GREEK TERMS

Horoskopoi, Greek term for priests whose task it was to know the details of the mythological and cultic calender.

Myein, Greek term meaning 'to close', from which 'mystery' was derived.

Oinercrites, Greek term for priestly dream interpreters.

Pteroforoi, Greek term for the *kheri hb* priests, the 'winged ones'.

Phyle, Greek term for the group of lay priests who served in the rotation.

Stolist, 'the priest of the private clothing', who was responsible for clothing the cult statue, called *medjty* or *chendjouty* by the Egyptians.

SELECTED
BIBLIOGRAPHY

Apuleius, Lucius, *The Golden Ass*, Penguin Classics, 1950.

Blackman, A.M., *Priest, Priesthood (Egyptian)* Encyclopaedia of Religion and Ethics 10, pp. 292–302. 1918.

—*Sequence of Episodes in the Egyptian Daily Temple Liturgy*, Manchester Egyptian and Oriental Society, pp. 48–52. 1918–19.

Bleeker, C.J., *Hathor and Thoth–Two Key Figures of the Ancient Egyptian Religion*, Brill, 1973.

—*Initiation in Ancient Egypt*, Brill, 1965.

Budge, W., *The Gods of the Egyptians*, 2 vols, Dover Publications, 1969.

Cook, R.J., *The Pyramids of Giza*, Seven Islands, 1992.

David, A.R., and Tapp, E., *The Mummy's Tale*, Michael O'Mara Books, 1992

David, R., *Religious Ritual at Abydos*, Aris and Phillips, 1973.

Davies, W.V. *Egyptian Hieroglyphs*, British Museum Publications, 1990.

Edwards, I.E.S., *The Pyramids of Egypt*, Pelican, 1977.

Engnell, I., *Studies in Divine Kingship in the Ancient Near East*, Blackwell, 1967.

Faulkner, R.O., *Book of the Dead*, British Museum Publications, 1972.

—'The Songs of Isis and Nephthys', *Journal of Egyptian Archaeology*, vol 22, pp.121–40, 1936.

—*The Ancient Egyptian Pyramid Texts*, Aris and Phillips, 1978.

Frankfort, H. *Kingship and the Gods*, University of Chicago Press, 1948.

Galvin, M., *The Priestesses of Hathor in the Old Kingdom and the First Intermediate Period*, Brandeis University Microfilm no. 8126877.

Griffiths, J.G., *The Conflict of Horus and Seth*, Liverpool University Press, 1960.

—*The Origins of Osiris and his Cult*, Brill, 1980.

Guthrie, K.S., *The Pythagorean Sourcebook*, Phanes Press, 1987.

Hart, G., *Pharaoh and Pyramids – A Guide Through Old Kingdom Egypt*, BCA, 1991.

Krupp, E.C., *In Search of Ancient Astronomies*, Doubleday, 1979.

Lamy, L., *Egyptian Mysteries*, Thames and Hudson, 1981.

Lichtheim, M., *Ancient Egyptian Literature*, 3 vols, University of California Press, 1973, 76, 80.

Lockyer, N., *The Dawn of Astronomy*, reprint MIT Press, 1973.

Lundquist, J.M., *The Temple – Meeting Place of Heaven and Earth*, Thames and Hudson, 1993.

Mahdy, el C., *Mummies, Myth and Magic*, Thames and Hudson, 1991.

Mercer, S.A.B., *Horus, The Royal God of Egypt*, Grafton, Mass., 1942.

Otto, E., *Egyptian Art and the Cult of Osiris and Amon*, Thames and Hudson, 1968.

Parker, R.A., *Ancient Egyptian Astronomy*, Philosophical Transactions of the Royal Society, Vol. 276, pp.51–65, 1974.

Plutarch, *Isis and Osiris* (Moralia Book 5) trans. J. Gwyn Griffiths, University of Wales Press, 1970.

Procter, R., *The Great Pyramid, Observatory Tomb and Temple* (nd).

Rice, M., *Egypt's Making, The Origins of Ancient Egypt*, Routledge, 1990.

Santiliana, G. de and Dechend, H. von, *Hamlet's Mill*, Godine, 1977.

Sauneron, S., *The Priests of Ancient Egypt*, trans. A. Morrissett, Pelican, 1960.

Schwaller de Lubicz, I., *The Opening of the Way*, Inner Traditions, 1979.

—*Her–Bak*, Vols 1, 11. Inner Traditions, 1967.

Schwaller de Lubicz, R.A., *The Egyptian Miracle*, Inner Traditions, 1949.

—*The Temple in Man*, Inner Traditions, 1949.

—*Sacred Science*, Inner Traditions, 1982.

Sellers, J., *The Death of Gods in Ancient Egypt*, Penguin, 1992.

Spence, L., *The Mysteries of Egypt*, Rider (nd).

Spencer, A.J., *Death in Ancient Egypt*, Pelican, 1982.

Wainwright, G.A., 'Seshat and the Pharaoh', *Journal of Egyptian Archaeology*, vol. 26, pp.30–40, 1940.

Wilkinson, R.H., *Reading Egyptian Art*, Thames and Hudson, 1992.

INDEX